BETH HILLEL LIBRARY

WITHDRAWN

Gift of the

Graduating Class of

1979

**KNOW YOUR FESTIVALS
AND ENJOY THEM**

KNOW YOUR FESTIVALS AND ENJOY THEM

The How and Why of the Jewish Festivals

BY
MORRIS GOLOMB

SECOND EDITION

SHENGOLD PUBLISHERS, INC.
NEW YORK

First Printing, 1973
Second Printing, 1976

Library of Congress Catalog Card Number: 72-90771

Published by Shengold Publishers, Inc., New York

Copyright © 1972 by Morris Golomb

All rights reserved

Printed in the United States of America

NOBLE OFFSET PRINTERS, INC.
New York, N.Y. 10003

Dedicated to our dear parents, Abraham and Taube Golomb and Rabbi Isaac and Michla Haft, who have implanted within us the everlasting life of Torah.

CONTENTS

The Sabbath	11
High Holidays Rosh HaShana and Yom Kippur	31
Sukkot	51
Hanukka	67
Tu Bishvat	81
Purim	91
Pesah	105
Israel Independence Day	119
Lag B'Omer	136
Shavuot	147
Fast Days	161
Rosh Hodesh	179
For Further Reading	183

INTRODUCTION

This volume on the Jewish festivals is an outgrowth of a series of individual booklets entitled THE HOW AND WHY for each festival. They were originally prepared as basic reading material for those of my students with whom I usually had little personal contact. However, it was soon discovered that not only the eight-to-twelve-year old youngsters for whom they had primarily been written but also many adults became interested in them and found much of value in their message. It was therefore found most feasible to publish them in a single volume.

This HOW AND WHY approach represents a distinct departure from that of most works on this popular subject. Its general objectives are as follows:

1. To set forth methodically some of the basic reasons underlying the observance of each festival in simple, concise and meaningful form.

2. To provide a brief description of the most common customs and ceremonies connected with each festival.

3. To arouse a desire on the part of the reader to participate in these observances as an integral part of full Jewish living (e.g., in the chapter on the Sabbath, "How About Observing the Sabbath").

4. Then, as an ultimate objective, to whet the appetite of the reader and stimulate him to delve more deeply into some of the classical sources of Jewish lore, referred to in this volume.

As for the last objective listed, let us remember that our festivals have always been connected with learning and study as well as rest, leisure and enjoyment. Thus, the Five Scrolls are to be read on each respective feast or fast day. Also, the commandment of *Vayakheyl* (Deuteronomy 31:9 ff.) instituted the public reading of the Law periodically. These and other examples demonstrate the vast potential value that knowledge of the festivals offers as a source of ongoing study of Jewish lore.

The general structure of each chapter is also unique in its dichotomized form of HOW AND WHY. Thus, as each festival is discussed, first comes the WHY, positing the reasons for its observance, and then the HOW, with its appropriate customs and ceremonies. Arbitrary as such a dichotomy may at first appear, an arrangement such as this enables the young reader to find the basic information he is seeking in the succinct form in which he desires to use it.

Therefore, although no attempt has been made at a thorough or exhaustive treatment of any one subject, nevertheless every vital aspect of each festival has been included, even though it may be only pin-pointed, leaving a fuller discussion to the additional reading as suggested by the bibliography.

It is hoped that the material provided in this volume will be of use, interest, and value to others than children. The summaries which follow some of the chapters may also be helpful as a review and a refresher.

The writer wishes to express his deep gratitude to all those who contributed to the culmination of this work and to make its publication possible. Special thanks are due to my devoted wife, Eve, whose timeless efforts in preparing the manuscripts have proved to be of invaluable assistance. Also, to all others who have given their inspiration and cooperation in one way or another—a hearty *Yasher Koach*.

Shvat, 5733
January, 1973   M.G.

THE SABBATH

Kiddush cup for Shabbat, designed by Peter Ehrenthal, New York.

On a busy city street, some years ago, a man once placed a gold coin on the sidewalk and then stood aside to see what would happen. Certain that the first of the hundreds of passersby would snatch it up, he was amazed to see, after some time had passed, how many people simply stopped, looked at the coin, and moved on. They were afraid to pick it up, fearing something tricky or suspicious might be involved. You may be sure however that, had the same coin been put in a place that was hard to reach, many of these same people would have gone after it without any hesitation or fear.

But, you yourself—have you ever realized that right in front of you, quite within easy reach, you have a valuable treasure waiting to be picked up? "What," you may ask, "is the rich prize within my reach?" It is the SABBATH! In fact, our rabbis tell us that the Sabbath was God's greatest gift to Israel. Indeed, we Jews have prized it for many centuries. In fact, as you will soon find out, it was the Sabbath that preserved us as Jews throughout all those centuries!

"But," you may wonder, "how can a single day be as valuable as all that when it comes week after week, 52 times every year? What is so valuable about that?"

On the surface that does seem strange. But on second thought we realize that it is because the Sabbath comes so often—and not only once a year as do all the other festivals—that we prize it so highly. What is more, strange as it may seem, the Sabbath day is the happiest day of the year! It comes every week to bring us joy as well as rest, to make our lives both happy and meaningful.

The following pages will explain HOW and WHY we observe the Sabbath. You will be told the reasons underlying many Sabbath observances, some of which are not always clearly understood. You will also learn the true meaning of such common terms as "rest" and "joy," because for us Jews, especially as regards the Sabbath, they have an entirely different meaning than the one you may have expected.

The HOW section briefly describes the various ways of keeping the Sabbath, from beginning to end. You will be shown exactly what to do as you observe this wonderful day of days. Then comes "How about Observing the Sabbath," where certain troubling questions or doubts you may have regarding the Sabbath are explained and answered.

Another useful feature is the "Terms for Sabbath," a handy guide defining names and terms you may not fully understand or whose meaning you may tend to forget. Test yourself on these and see how many you know.

A few Zemirot (Sabbath hymns) too have been included to help you sing them during your Sabbath meals.

At the end of this book is a list of materials recommended "For Further Reading." This includes of course only a selection of the many books written about the Sabbath. Many other titles may be found in Abraham Millgram's *Sabbath, the Day of Delight*, which is included in our list. A number of these may be available at your school, center, or public library. Reading a few of these, as well as the Bible selections, will give you a much better and more thorough understanding of the meaning of the Sabbath.

Our Sages taught that the Sabbath was given us to enjoy. Let us then double, treble, and quadruple our enjoyment of the Sabbath, both by learning more about it and by observing it. Make Sabbath a delight by finding out what hidden treasures it has in store for you. The pleasure will be all yours.

SHABBAT SHALOM!

THE WHY OF THE SABBATH

The Sabbath is the holiest day of the year, despite its occurring 52 successive times. It is not only a sacred day but also one filled with joy and delight. For thousands of years it has been the happiest as well as the holiest day in the Jewish calendar.

What is more, the Sabbath has been responsible for keeping the Jew alive throughout all those years. Yet many obstacles and difficulties interfered. Why then do we still observe it so regularly today? How has all this been possible? To find the answer, let us examine a few of the basic reasons for keeping the Sabbath.

First and foremost, we must go back to the Bible. There we are told that after the six days of creation God rested on the seventh day, making that day holy. Thus the Sabbath began. It is believed that the Sabbath observance constitutes one of the earliest Jewish laws. Later, in the Ten Commandments, we find that the fourth one strictly forbids doing any work on the Sabbath, commanding us to rest on that day, because God Himself rested on the seventh day. In fact, this commandment is the only one of the ten which tells us exactly how to observe it— a fact which proves its sanctity and its importance for us Jews.

The Bible states additional reasons for observing the Sabbath. One is to remind us of the exodus from Egypt. It is believed that even during their slavery in Egypt the Israelites observed the Sabbath.

Further on we read that while journeying through the desert on their way to the Promised Land the Israelites were forbidden to pick the manna (the food eaten while in the desert) on the Sabbath. Instead, they were instructed to gather a double portion of manna on Friday—which is the reason we place two loaves of halla on the table for our Sabbath dinner.

Other laws for the Sabbath observance were added in later periods, both by the Prophets who came after Moses and by the scribes and scholars who explained to the people many of the laws of the Bible, after that great Book had already been completed. The purpose of these laws was not only to make the Biblical injunctions easier to understand and to observe, but also to make Jewish observances more livable, enjoyable and meaningful.

Thus, for example, since the Torah forbids the use of fire on the Sabbath, the Rabbis interpreted this to mean that no fire should be lighted for heating food on the Sabbath day, nor should any light be kindled for illumination, but that a fire started before the Sabbath could be used to warm Sabbath food, and that light kindled prior to the Sabbath could be used on the holy day.

Now, it is not only because the Bible commands us to keep the Sabbath that we Jews observe it, but also because it is a day which is special and significant in and of itself. "All right," you may ask, "but what is so special about it?" Many things—here are just a few.

As has already been mentioned, it is a day of complete rest for body and mind. On this day the Jew throws off all weekday toil and worry and devotes his thoughts and deeds to higher, more uplifting matters. In other words, he becomes a different person than he has been during the previous six days.

But, at the same time, rest does not mean just idleness or laziness. The purpose of Sabbath rest is to free yourself for devotion to some of those activities that are proper only for the Sabbath day. How can you tell what is proper for Sabbath? To understand this better let us first examine some of those loftier, deeper thoughts and provide the reason for observing Sabbath as we should and for behaving as we should on that holiest of all days.

Perhaps the most important of all these nobler thoughts is that during the entire day of Sabbath we place our full faith in God alone. This means that when we stop all our week-day work, we rely upon God to take care of us throughout the Sabbath. In this way we show that we remember that the Lord also rested on that day. Or, to put it another way, if you do not observe the Sabbath, you show God that you have little faith in Him to look after you for that one day.

Now, in addition to rest, the Sabbath brings us joy. The happiness which the Sabbath gives is not the joy of the moment, that is, the kind of pleasure that comes and goes and then leaves you as bored and unhappy as ever. Instead, when you rejoice on the Sabbath you carry that joy with you throughout the rest of the week. (The different ways of expressing such joy will be presented in the HOW section). In fact, in order to make sure that you will be happy and joyful on the Sabbath, any sign of sadness or mourning is forbidden. No other day of the week can make your joy so complete.

Still another mark of the Sabbath day is its sense of equality. On that day every Jew is the equal of his fellow man, whether he be richer or poorer, higher or lower, more learned or less learned, better or worse in any other way. The day of Sabbath thus gives every Jew who observes it, without exception, the opportunity to be like a prince among men by resting from all works, eating better than on week days, dressing better, rejoicing, and in many other ways. According to the fourth commandment, even one's servants and working animals must rest on the Sabbath. This makes it clear to the Jew that God made all beings equal, that is, with equal rights.

During the dark days of persecution which so many Jews of various countries and various epochs had to suffer, the Jew always had the Sabbath to look forward to each week as an escape from his daily troubles. Even under conditions of peace, freedom and justice that many of us enjoy today, the Sabbath still refreshes our souls, giving us new hope to overcome the difficult moments of the week. Rested, happy, and inspired by the Sabbath's delights, we are ready once more to face life's problems with renewed faith and courage.

In addition, the Sabbath is also intended to be a day of learning, study and prayer. Being rested and more relaxed, we can enjoy learning and prayer so much more on the Sabbath day. The HOW section includes several examples of prayer and study for the Sabbath day.

HOW WE OBSERVE THE SABBATH

Traditionally, the Jew pictures the Sabbath as a special "guest" whose coming calls for careful plans and preparations. This guest is popularly known as a "Queen"—The Sabbath Queen—lovely and beautiful as a bride. Therefore, in honor of the coming of "Queen Sabbath" we must begin preparations in advance.

First, however, let us remember that the Jew is mindful of the Sabbath not only on the Sabbath itself, and not merely a few days before, but actually every day of the week. For the six week days are known not by name, but by number. The first day of the week days is called the "First Day." Its full name should really be "The First Day Towards Sabbath." Next come the Second Day, the Third Day, etc. Thus named, each day indicates precisely how many days away is the Sabbath.

As noted above, a day or two before the Sabbath begins, the housewife starts her preparations by buying all the food, cleaning the house, and making sure the clothing—holiday finery—is in good order. To honor that day only the best food and drinks are served and the best clothes worn. All the cooking and baking is done well in advance since such work is, of course, forbidden on the day of rest. At the same time the house and furniture, the silver and glassware are cleaned and polished in honor of this holy day.

Consequently, Friday, known as *Erev Shabbat* (Sabbath Eve), is a busy day in the Jewish home. By noon all the food has been prepared, the house is spic-and-span and the entire household is getting ready to welcome the Sabbath Queen. Early in the afternoon everyone stops the week's work.

The honor of ushering in the Sabbath is given to the mother of the house: she lights the Sabbath candles (not less than two) about half an hour before sundown, reciting the special blessing over them. No work is permitted once the candles have been lighted.

By this time the father and the sons have already left for the synagogue. There, the first set of prayers to be recited are the special ones known as *Kabbalat Shabbat* (Welcoming the Sabbath). The well-known tune, *L'cha Dodi*, is sung during this part of the service. Then follows the Evening Service, which includes special portions for the Sabbath. At the close of the service the cantor chants the *Kiddush* prayer over the wine. The Sabbath greeting *Shabbat Shalom* in Hebrew, or *Gut Shabbos* in Yiddish, are exchanged by all, both in the synagogue and in the home.

As soon as the father and his sons enter the house upon their return from the synagogue, following the exchange of the Sabbath greetings, all join in singing the familiar hymn *Shalom Aleichem*, in which we welcome the angels of the Sabbath. (Two angels, one good and one bad, are believed to accompany the father home from the synagogue.) The father now blesses his children by placing his hands over their heads and reciting the blessing. The spirit of Sabbath, which Queen Sabbath has brought into the home, is felt by every member of the family and any guests present.

The table is set in honor of the Queen. On a white tablecloth stand the candlesticks with their glowing candles. At the head of the table are two braided loaves (hallas) covered with a white or embroidered napkin. Beside these is father's silver Kiddush cup. Only the best dishes, linen and silverware are used.

Around this table the entire family stands as the father chants the Kiddush prayer. This prayer contains two of the many reasons for observing the Sabbath—first, as a reminder of the creation, and second for the exodus from Egypt. The Kiddush finished, everyone present tastes a bit of wine.

Then follows the first of the three meals which every Jew must have on the Sabbath. (Fasting is forbidden on the Sabbath, except on Yom Kippur.) After the special washing of the hands, the hallas are broken and the father, followed by all the others, recites the *Ha-Motzi* (the blessing over the bread, which marks the beginning of every meal). The hearty and appetizing meal that is then served usually includes such traditional delicacies as gefilte fish (stuffed fish), chicken noodle soup, roast meat or chicken, kugel (pudding) and other mouth-watering treats. Between courses certain special hymns, called *Zemirot*, are sung in unison. The meal ends with the recitation of *Birkat Ha-Mazon* (Grace after meals).

During the remainder of the evening everyone rests, reading, relaxing, chatting. Some may visit friends or relatives. The father of the house then reviews the *Sedra* (special Torah portion) of the week, going over it three times, twice in the Hebrew (with the commentaries that explain it) and once in the Aramaic translation. It is also customary for him to discuss with the children their Hebrew studies of the week.

Sabbath morning finds the entire family in the synagogue, where special Sabbath prayers are added to those recited during week-day services.

Then comes the Torah service. Amidst special prayers and singing the Torah scroll is taken from the Ark and read by the *Baal Korey* (the Torah reader). Seven or more men are called to the Torah one by one for an *Aliyah*, the honor of being called up to the Torah to witness the reading of a portion of the weekly *Sedra* (Torah portion). At the conclusion of the seven Aliyot comes the *Maftir*, the man called to read the *Haftorah* which is a portion taken from the books of the Prophets. This is the most honored of all the Aliyot. If a boy celebrating his Bar Mitzva is participating in the service, he is accorded the honor of reading the Haftorah portion.

Returning home from the synagogue, the family is ready for the second main Sabbath meal. Following a short Kiddush recited by the father, another appetizing full-course meal is served. Again, Zemirot are sung—this time even more than on Friday evening.

The afternoon is once more a period devoted to rest, relaxation, play, and study. Later in the day a rabbi or scholar may be preaching at the synagogue. The *Minha* (afternoon) service then follows. Again the Torah is read, but this time only a smaller portion.

The third and final meal of the Sabbath is then eaten. This meal, called the *Seudah Sh'lishit* (The Third Meal) is a light one. Now too Zemirot are sung.

Just as the Sabbath queen was given a royal welcome upon her arrival on Friday evening, so is she now given a grand send-off as she is about to depart. This ceremony is known as the *Havdala* (separation) service. In conducting it the following objects are used: a braided candle with four wicks, a cup of wine (or any other suitable social drink), and a *Besamim* (spice) box.

As the candle is lighted, the father recites the Havdala prayer and the blessings over the candle, the wine and the spices. During the blessing over the candle he holds his fingers, curved, near the flame. In the Havdala prayer we ask for a good week, as we are now ready to resume the work forbidden on the Sabbath. Following this ceremony all present respond GUT WOCH! in Yiddish (a happy week) or SHAVUA TOV! in Hebrew. In fact, during this Havdala service we seek to begin the new week by exercising our five senses in the following manner: we SEE the lighted candle; we HEAR the prayer; we TASTE the wine; we SMELL the spices; and we FEEL the heat of the flame.

But although the Sabbath is over, its holy atmosphere continues to linger for some time. It is therefore also customary for some highly-observant Jews to conduct a *Melavah Malkah*, a special celebration held Saturday night and featuring songs, stories and general merriment.

Havdala set.

SPECIAL SABBATHS

During the year the following special Sabbaths are observed:

1. *Shabbat M'varchim*, the Sabbath before the New Moon, whose coming during that week is then announced. *Mevor'chim* means "blessing" (of the new moon).

2. *Shabbat Ha-Gadol* (the great Sabbath), which comes just before Passover.

3. *Shabbat Hazon*, the Sabbath before the Fast of Ab. Its name is taken from the opening word of the Haftorah, *Hazon* (Isaiah, 1:1), in which the prophet reprimands the people for their many sins.

4. *Shabbat Nachamu*, the Sabbath following the Fast of Ab. Its name comes from the Haftora's opening word, *Nachamu* ("Comfort"), which is followed by words of comfort and cheer, as spoken by Isaiah (40:1).

5. *Shabbat Shira* (the Sabbath of Song), the Sabbath before Tu Bishvat. The song referred to is the hymn of praise to God sung by the Israelites following the miracle of the Red Sea.

6. *Shabbat Shuva* (the Sabbath of Repentance), which comes between Rosh HaShana and Yom Kippur. This Sabbath also derives its name from the opening word of the Haftorah, *Shuva* ("repent" or "return") (Hosea, 14:2). The rabbi usually delivers a High Holiday sermon during that afternoon.

BLESSINGS, PRAYERS AND HYMNS
FOR SHABBAT EVE

Lighting the Shabbat Candles:
Ba-ruch A-tah Ado-nay, Elo-hay-nu Me-lech Ha-o-lam, a-sher Kid-sha-nu B'mitz-vo-tav V'tzi-va-nu, L'had-leek nayr shel Shabbat.

* * * * *

To be sung before reciting the Kiddush:

1. Sha-lom al-eichem, mal-a-chay ha'sha-rayt, mal-a-chay, el-yon Mi-me-lech, ma-l'chay ha-m'la-chim, Ha-ka-dosh Ba-ruch Hoo.

2. Bo-a-chem l'sha-lom, mal-a-chay ha-sha-lom, mal-a-chay el-yon Mi-me-lech, ma-l'chay ha-m'la-chim, Ha-ka-dosh Ba-ruch Hoo.

3. Bar-chu-ni l'sha-lom, mal-a-chay ha-sha-lom, mal-a-chay el-yon Mi-me-lech, ma-l'chay ha-m'la-chim, Ha-ka-dosh Ba-ruch Hoo.

4. Tzayt-chem l'sha-lom, mal-a-chay ha-sha-lom, mal-a-chay el-yon Mi-me-lech, ma-l'chay ha-m'la-chim, Ha-ka-dosh Ba-ruch Hoo.

* * * * *

Blessing over the Wine:
Ba-ruch A-tah A-do-nay Elo-hay-nu Me-lech Ha-o-lam, Bo-ray P'ree Ha-ga-fen.

* * * * *

Blessing over the Halla (Bread):
Ba-ruch A-tah A-do-nay Elo-hay-nu Me-lech Ha-o-lam, Ha–motzi Le-chem Min Ha-a-retz.

* * * * *

SABBATH HYMNS

Ya-ri-bon O-lam V'ol-ma-yah, Ahnt-hoo Mal-kah, Me-lech mal-cha-ya
O-vad g'voor-teych v'tim-ha-yah, sh'far ka-da'may, l'hah-va-yah
Ya-ri-bon O-lam V'ol-ma-yah, Ahnt-hoo Mal-kah, Me-lech mal-cha-ya.

* * * * *

Tzur mee-she-loh a-chal-nu, ba-r'choo emu-nye, sa-vah-noo v'ho-tar-noo Ki-d'var A-do-nay.
Ha-zan et o-la-mo ro-ay-noo a-vee-noo, a-chal-nu et lach-mo,
V'aya-no sha-tee-noo, al kayn no-deh li-shmo, u-n'ha-l'lo b'fee-noo,
A-mar-noo v'a-nee-noo, ayn, ka-dosh ka-do-noy.
Tzur mee-she-lo a-chal-nu, bar-r'choo emu-nye, sa-vah-noo v'ho-tar-noo Ki-d'var A-do-nay.

HOW ABOUT OBSERVING THE SABBATH?

We have just read what *WE* must do *FOR* the Sabbath day. This section will tell us just the opposite—what the Sabbath can do *FOR US!* What can just one day of every week do for the Jew? Can you measure the new and refreshed vigor and energy that fill every Jew who observes the Sabbath properly? What magic power does this holy day possess? Great thinkers and scholars of other nations have marveled at the Jew as they asked these questions.

But there is no secret involved. The Jew observes his Sabbath because to him it is a special day unlike any other.* Moreover, here in America, it is possible to keep the Sabbath since most of us work only five days a week which leaves us free on the Sabbath day.

In Israel the Sabbath is observed by the nation as a whole, since that day is its official day of rest (just as Sunday is in the United States and other Christian lands, and just as Friday is in the Moslem countries). Most stores, offices, and industries are closed on that day and, with a few exceptions, the majority of the Jews rest on that day.

During a recent visit, this writer was especially impressed with the way Sabbath is observed in Israel, particularly in Jerusalem. The calm and the contentment which one feels as he sees streets filled with worshippers walking to and from synagogue, the sound of Zemirot issuing from all sides, the bright glow of candles seen in every home on Friday night, the aroma of Sabbath delicacies—all of these sensations transport one into a world of joy and delight. At the Western Wall hundreds of people gather for Sabbath worship. Elsewhere throughout Israel most Jews observe the Sabbath in similar ways. To see such a full observance of the Sabbath is an experience never to be forgotten.

But for us in America there is much we can do to observe and beautify the Sabbath. For one thing, we must learn more about what Sabbath means and what to do to observe it properly. The more we know, the more we will understand. A beginning has already been made in what we have said here. We hope you will read a good deal more in the books listed in "For Further Reading."

In this connection let us remember the wise saying of Ahad Ha'am, a famous Jewish scholar who lived several decades ago. In one of his books Ahad Ha'am declared, "More than the Jew has kept the Sabbath, the Sabbath has kept the Jew!" In other words, observing the Sabbath helped the Jew to remain a Jew and made him a happier, healthier, and more contented person. The more we put into being Jews, the more we are rewarded as Jews. That is why the Jew loves and treasures his Judaism.

Throughout our long history, whether in ancient, modern, or more recent times (yes, even during our present day) Jews everywhere have struggled, fought, and sacrificed to observe the Sabbath—at times, even giving their lives for that holy day! Happily, we need not go through all of this. We are not called upon to do the impossible. We need only to convince ourselves that we really WANT to be Sabbath observers, and then—"Where there's a will, there's a way!"

So if you are not already a Sabbath observer, HOW ABOUT OBSERVING THE SABBATH? You are in for a rare treat!

---

* Read the story "The Sabbath Taste" in A. Millgram's *Sabbath, The Day of Delight*, pp. 105-8. It is also found in S.R. Weilerstein's *What the Moon Brought*, pp. 55-62. Both these books are listed under "For Further Reading."

TERMS FOR THE SABBATH

ALIYAH	An honor of being called up to the Torah while it is being read (The term is also used to mean the immigration of a Jew to Israel)
ARAMAIC	An ancient language akin to Hebrew used in some prayers and also in rabbinic literature
BESAMIM	Spices used during the *Havdala* service
BIRKAT HA-MAZON	The Grace-after-meals prayer
CHOLENT	A favorite Sabbath food that is kept warm during the Sabbath until served
COVENANT	An agreement, usually one made between man and God
EREV SHABBAT	The day before, or the eve of, Sabbath
EXODUS	The departure of the Israelites from Egypt. Also, the name of the second of the Five Books of Moses
FOURTH COMMANDMENT	"Remember the Sabbath day to keep it holy" (Read the rest of it in your Bible in Exodus 20:9-11)
GEFILTE FISH	"Stuffed fish"—a favorite Sabbath dish
"GUT WOCH"	"A good week!"—the greeting marking the end of the Sabbath
HAFTORAH	The portion from the Books of the Prophets that is read at the conclusion of the Torah reading on Sabbaths and Festivals
HALLA	The twisted loaves of white bread for Sabbaths and Festivals
HA-MOTZI	The blessing said over the bread
HAVDALA	"Separation"—The service on Saturday night bidding farewell to the Sabbath
HAVDALA CANDLE	A special candle with four wicks, used for the Havdala service on Saturday night
KABBALAT SHABBAT	"Welcoming the Sabbath"—A set of prayers said just before the evening service on Sabbath eve

23

KIDDUSH	"Sanctification" (making holy) — A prayer said before the Sabbath or Festival meal
K'RIAT HA-TORAH	"Reading of the Torah," the Torah service
KUGEL	A pudding served for the Sabbath meals
L'CHA DODI	One of the principal hymns of the "Kabbalat Shabbat" service of Sabbath eve
MANNA	The food the Israelites ate while wandering in the wilderness for 40 years
MELAVAH MALKAH	A Saturday night celebration for the departing Sabbath
MINHA	The afternoon service
MOTZAEY SHABBAT	The "departure of the Sabbath"
MUSSAF	The Additional Service recited on Sabbath and Festivals following the reading of the Torah
ONEG SHABBAT	"Sabbath joy". A party or meeting held on the Sabbath for expressing Sabbath joy through songs, dances, talks, refreshments, and the like
PROPHETS	"Men of God" in Bible times who could communicate with God and who taught the people God's ways
ROSH CHODESH BENTCHEN	The "blessing of the new month," that is, the coming month
ROSH HODESH	The beginning of each new month
SEDRA	The weekly Torah portion that is read on the Sabbath
SEUDAH SH'LISHIT	The "Third Meal," eaten during late Sabbath afternoon
SHABBAT M'VARCHIM	The Sabbath when the blessing of the coming month takes place
SHABBAT SHALOM	"Sabbath of Peace"! "Good Sabbath"—a Sabbath greeting
SHACHARIT	The name of the morning service
SHALOM ALEICHEM	Name of a Sabbath hymn welcoming the Angels of the Sabbath

SHOMER SHABBAT	A Sabbath observer
(The) TWO ANGELS	The "good" and the "bad" angels who visit every Jewish home on Sabbath eve
TZIMMES	A Sabbath food usually made of sweetened cooked carrots
ZEMIROT	Sabbath (or festival) hymns sung at the table

NUMBERS RELATED TO THE SABBATH

1 Sabbath lasts but *one* day

2 The *two* Hallas used on the Sabbath

3 The *three* Meals of the Sabbath
   Three stars must appear before Sabbath is declared to be over

4 The *Fourth* Commandment, which orders us to observe the Sabbath

5 The *Five* Books of Moses

6 Friday, the *sixth* day of the week, is Erev Shabbat
   God created the world in *six* days

7 Sabbath comes on the *seventh* day
   No less than *seven* men are called to the Torah on the Sabbath

10 The *Ten* Commandments

22 Sabbath must begin no later than about *22* minutes before sundown

54 The Torah is divided into *54* Sedrot, or weekly Torah portions

QUIZ QUESTIONS ON THE SABBATH

QUESTIONS: *ANSWERS:*

1. Which of the Ten Commandments tells us to observe the Sabbath?

1. The fourth

2. In which way does the Fourth Commandment differ from the other nine?

2. It is the only one which tells how it is to be observed

3. Why must everyone rest on the Sabbath?

3. Because on this day God rested from all His work

4. Tell whether on the Sabbath we are expected to be:
a) sad; b) serious; c) happy; or, d) free to act as we please

4. c) Happy

5. Compared to other festivals the Sabbath is:
a) less important; b) just as important; c) more important; d) none of these

5. c) More important

6. For what two reasons does the Fourth Commandment tell us to observe the Sabbath?

6. a) God rested on that day
b) As a reminder of our release from Egyptian bondage

7. a) How many regular meals are to be eaten on the Sabbath?
b) Tell when each is eaten.

7. a) Three
b) Friday evening, Sabbath noon, late Sabbath afternoon

8. I am the Sabbath Queen. Name a few ways in which you prepare to greet me.

8. a) Prepare good food
b) Clean the house
c) Dress better than usual
d) Stop work earlier on Friday

9. a) What are Hallas?
b) How many are usually placed on the Sabbath table?
c) What is the reason for that number?

9. a) Twisted white loaves eaten on Sabbath reminding us of the shew bread used during Temple times
b) Two
c) To remind us of the double portion of Manna which the Israelites gathered on Fridays during the days of their wandering in the wilderness

10. On Friday the Sabbath must begin
    a) Sometime before sundown.
    b) Just before sundown.
    c) At sundown.
    d) After sundown.

11. Sabbath actually begins with
    a) Reciting the Kiddush.
    b) Lighting the candles.
    c) Going to the synagogue.
    d) Beginning the Sabbath meal.

12. We first welcome the Sabbath with the prayer
    a) Shalom Aleichem.
    b) Adon Olam.
    c) L'cha Dodi.
    d) Shabbat Shalom.

13. Who is to accompany a Jew home as he returns from synagogue on Friday night?

14. I am the prayer recited just before the Friday evening meal. Who am I?

15. Name at least two foods usually served during the Sabbath meal.

16. What are Zemirot?

17. How many times does the father usually read the Sedra of the week?

18. During which part of the service is the Torah Scroll read in the synagogue?

19. How many men are called to the Torah on Sabbath morning?

20. I am the Hebrew name for the weekly portion of the Torah. Name me.

10. a) Sometime before sundown (about 22 minutes after candle-lighting time)

11. b) Lighting the candles

12. c) L'cha Dodi

13. Two angels

14. The Kiddush

15. Fish, chicken soup, chicken, pudding, tzimmes

16. Hymns sung during the Sabbath meal

17. Three times; twice in the Hebrew and once in the Aramaic translation

18. Between the Shacharit and Mussaf services

19. Seven or more

20. Sedra, or Parshah

21. The portion from the Prophets usually read by a Bar Mitzvah boy is called the ———.

21. Haftorah

22. I am the last regular meal eaten on Sabbath. Who am I?

22. Seudah Sh'lishit, or the Third Meal, which is eaten towards the close of the Sabbath Day

23. With which ceremony does the Sabbath day end?

23. Havdala

24. We are three objects used during the Havdala service. Can you name us?

24. Lighting candle; wine (or some other permissible liquid) and spices

25. Why is the Havdala service necessary?

25. a) To show that we are dividing the Sabbath from the weekdays
b) To bid farewell to the Sabbath

26. How are the five senses put to use during the Havdala service?

26. a) We *see* the lighted candle
b) We *hear* the Havdala prayer
c) We *feel* the heat of the flame
d) We *taste* the wine
e) We *smell* the spices

27. In which way is a Havdala candle different from any other candle?

27. It must have more than one wick

28. Sabbath has just ended. What is the sign for this?

28. When you can see at least three stars in the sky

29. Sabbath ends
a) Just before dark.
b) Right at dark.
c) After stars have appeared.
d) After Havdala.

29. c) After stars have appeared in the sky

30. Melavah Malkah is my name. Who am I?

30. A special ceremony of eating and drinking and merrymaking after Havdala

31. How is Sabbath afternoon usually spent?

31. Resting, studying, visiting, participating in an *Oneg Shabbat* gathering

32. What do all the following have in common?
   Shabbat Shira
   Shabbat Shuva
   Shabbat Ha-Gadol

32. They are all some of the special Sabbaths of the year

33. What is important about each of the following Sabbaths?
    a) Shabbat Ha-Gadol
    b) Shabbat Hazon
    c) Shabbat Nachamu
    d) Shabbat Shira
    e) Shabbat Shuva
    f) Shabbat M'vorchim

33. a) Shabbat Ha-Gadol; Sabbath before Passover
    b) Shabbat Hazon; Sabbath before 9th of Av
    c) Shabbat Nachamu; Sabbath after 9th of Av
    d) Shabbat Shira; Sabbath before Tu Bishvat
    e) Shabbat Shuva; Sabbath between Rosh HaShana and Yom Kippur
    f) Shabbat M'vorchim; Shabbat when the coming month is announced

34. How many times a year can Shabbat M'vorchim come? Why that number?

34. Eleven
    Because there is no blessing of the month during the month of Tishri

35. The two *main* reasons for resting on the Sabbath are
    a) To have more strength to work during the coming week.
    b) To have one day in which to relax and idle around.
    c) To spend the day in prayer and thinking about God.
    d) Because the Bible commands us to, so that we may rest properly.
    e) To show that you are a different kind of person than you are during the week.

35. d) Because the Bible commands us to, so that we may rest properly
    e) To show that you are a different kind of person than you are during the week

36. What was so special about the Covenant made between God and Israel?

36. God made that Covenant only with Israel—not with any other people

37. How does the Sabbath morning service in the synagogue differ from that of the weekdays?

37. The services are longer because additional prayers are added; a full Torah portion is read; a Haftorah is recited; there is a Mussaf service; the Rabbi usually delivers a sermon

38. a) Can you quote Ahad Ha'am's comment about the Sabbath?
b) What did he mean by that?

38. a) "More than the Jew has kept the Sabbath, the Sabbath has kept the Jew."
b) It is because the Jew has kept the Sabbath that the Sabbath has made him happier, healthier, and a better and more loyal Jew

39. What above all is required for one to be a good Sabbath observer?

39. A strong will, a deep love for the Sabbath, and the desire to observe it properly

ROSH HASHANA

When the High Holy Days come (usually during September or October) you see more Jews flocking to the synagogue than at any other time during the year. In fact, attendance at synagogues at that time is greater than during all other holidays put together! Why is it that Jews attend in such vast numbers on the High Holy Days only?

Most Jews who observe only Rosh HaShana and Yom Kippur and not other holidays of the year do so because they sense the seriousness and importance of these days in the life of every Jew.

The synagogue services are usually longer and more solemn than on all other holidays. Some people are puzzled by the meaning and significance of the holidays and the prayers. But these are not hard to learn. We bring the main facts about Rosh HaShana and Yom Kippur in this chapter.

We do not, however, mean to leave the impression that this is all there is to know about these holidays. To know all would be impossible. Even the great Rabbis and Sages of the Talmud never claimed to know all the answers to the meaning of the High Holy Days.

The HOW and WHY portions present information that should be very useful to you—but only as a beginning. We hope you will seek further information by reading the books listed under "For Further Reading," and others. Then every ceremony performed in the synagogue (as well as at home) will take on new meaning for you. Only in this way will you be able to feel as you should during the High Holy Days—sorry for any misdeeds of the past year and ready and willing to do better during the coming year.

L'SHANAH TOVAH TIKATEYVU! MAY YOU BE INSCRIBED
FOR A GOOD YEAR!

THE WHY OF THE HIGH HOLY DAYS

Most of our Jewish festivals are happy ones but a few days of the year are solemn and serious instead. That is why they are called the *High Holy Days*, or the *Solemn Days*.

"But" you may ask, "what is it that makes these days so solemn (or serious)?" It is our special concern during these days for our personal lives and for our ways of living that makes us examine ourselves more seriously than on other festivals. In other words, during these Solemn Days we realize that our very lives are hanging in the balance before God. Isn't that sufficient reason to become very serious?

Next, which are the High Holy Days? They extend over a period of ten days, and are also known as the Ten Days of Penitence. However, it is only the first two of them, *Rosh HaShana* (the New Year), and the last day, *Yom Kippur* (Day of Atonement), that are observed as major festivals. Each of these will be taken up separately. (As a matter of fact, the preparation for the High Holy Days begins some time before their arrival, as is true of certain other festivals.)

The basic reason for observing the High Holy Days is to examine the relations between man and God and between man and man more closely. Both Rosh HaShana and Yom Kippur achieve this purpose in their own special ways. We will see how this is done as we discuss them in the WHY and the HOW sections.

Tashlikh on a Tel Aviv Beach.

THE TEN DAYS OF PENITENCE

The period from Rosh HaShana through Yom Kippur consists of ten days, known as the *Aseret Y'mey T'shuvah* (Ten Days of Penitence). ("Penitence" means "feeling sorry.") However, as we have already seen, it is only Rosh HaShana and Yom Kippur that are observed as major holidays. The seven days between these two are meant to be the time when we seek to better our conduct so that in the Book of Life, in which our fate for the coming year is inscribed, God will write a favorable verdict for all of us.

WHY ROSH HASHANA

Rosh HaShana (which means "head of the year") is commonly known as the New Year, because our new year officially begins with the Hebrew month of Tishri, on the first and second days of that month. However, although the new year begins with Tishri, that month is actually the seventh month of the year, while Nissan (when Passover comes) is the first of the months.

As the new year begins, thus God judges us for the coming year. That is why this holiday is also known as *Yom Ha-Din* ("The Day of Judgment"). But, in order to judge us fairly and justly, God remembers and weighs all our acts of the past year before He gives His final verdict for each of us. For this reason Rosh HaShana is also known as *Yom Ha-Zikaron* ("The Day of Remembrance").

Now, in the Torah (the Five Books of Moses) Rosh HaShana is not known by any of these names. Instead, it commands us to observe it as *Yom T'ruah* ("The Day of Sounding the Shofar"). That is the fourth name given to Rosh HaShana (Leviticus, 23:24; Numbers, 29:1).

During Bible times the shofar (a ram's horn, one of the oldest musical instruments) was blown to announce an important and special event, as well as for certain other purposes. The beginning of the New Year was certainly important enough to be announced by the blast of the shofar. For this reason we remember this custom during the shofar service on Rosh HaShana. This is described in the HOW portion to follow.

And what does the shofar do for us today? Let us mention only a few things we can gain from hearing its blasts. First, the shofar serves as a constant reminder of several great events in our history for which it was sounded. The best-known and most significant was, of course, the giving of the Ten Commandments on Mount Sinai, when the shofar was sounded before and after this historic event.

It also brings to mind the Temple of old where the shofar was part of the service. Going even further back into history, the shofar first came to be known as a result of the story of Abraham's attempted sacrifice of his son Isaac, when God later ordered him to sacrifice a ram instead. Finally, the shofar reminds us of God's promise to redeem or free our people and enable them to return to Israel, the land of our fathers, where peace and freedom will come for everyone, Jews and non-Jews alike.

But, in addition to all these reasons, the shofar acts somewhat as a bugle does to a soldier, calling us to action. We, however, are not called to fight but to improve our conduct.

In short, we might refer to Rosh HaShana as a festival dealing with our past, present and future. On Rosh HaShana God not only recalls our deeds of the past year, but also hears our pleas to remember the righteous deeds of our forefathers for our sakes.

In the present, God judges our conduct, weighing it on the scale of justice—also on Rosh HaShana. Finally, Rosh HaShana also represents our hope for the future, because according to our Rabbis, it will be on this day that Israel will become fully free as a nation under God, on its own holy soil.

In this way Rosh HaShana reminds us to DIRECT our thoughts and deeds to God at all times, regarding our past, present and future, and gives us reason to hope as we seek to enrich and improve our lives.

THE WHY OF YOM KIPPUR

To show God that we sincerely plan to better our conduct during the coming year, we have to prove it by our deeds. That is why on Yom Kippur we observe certain laws and customs by means of which we seek to convince Him that we really deserve to be inscribed in the Book of Life. Since on this sacred day the Book of Life is closed and sealed until the next year, we perform these Yom Kippur observances to beg for life during the coming year, relying upon the Almighty's divine mercy to grant it to us. This is the basic reason for Yom Kippur's being the holiest day of the year.

Why we observe certain laws and customs on Yom Kippur will be mentioned here, but how they are observed will be discussed in the HOW section.

The principal laws which command us to observe Yom Kippur are mentioned in only a few places in the Torah, namely in the Book of Leviticus, 23:27-32, and in Numbers, 29:7-11. In addition, the ceremonies to be performed in the Temple by the High Priest during Yom Kippur day are set forth in Leviticus, 16:2-34. Thus, Yom Kippur is an official Biblically ordered holy day.

One of the most fundamental reasons for observing Yom Kippur is to ask for forgiveness for our sins. In fact, the Hebrew words *Yom Kippur* mean day of forgiveness (or atonement), which is another way of saying that we are truly sorry for having sinned. But to say that we are sorry is not enough. We must also do something to atone or correct the wrongs we did.

The forgiveness we ask is for both kinds of sins, those against God and those against man. The sins against God may be atoned in two ways: by praying and by fasting. But sins committed against man can only be forgiven by the person sinned against, not by God. And it is up to each one of us to take care of this personally.

Yom Kippur is also a day of fasting. We fast in order to be constantly reminded of the seriousness of this day and of what it means to our lives. In the Torah, fasting is stringently commanded as a basic observance of Yom Kippur. This is the first step in convincing God that we yearn to be forgiven. Praying is another such step. Therefore, on Yom Kippur, as on Rosh HaShana, we recite more prayers than usual and in some of these prayers we confess our sins.

Now, in Judaism, confession of sins has an entirely different meaning than it has in other religions. In the HOW section we will explain more thoroughly; here let us only mention that confession is another way of expressing our sincerity before God. Before we can ask Him to forgive any of our sins, we must first confess them. Furthermore, since Jews feel a close responsibility to one another, we say in our confession prayers, *We have sinned* instead of *I have sinned*.

In these three ways, then, by fasting, by praying and by confessing our sins—we try to show God that we are indeed sorry for having sinned and we thereby prove how sincere we are at this critical moment.

However, the main purpose of these three acts is to help us improve our conduct during the new year and thus to approach closer to God. Then when the Book of Life closes at the end of Yom Kippur, we will feel more confident that it will be sealed with a favorable verdict inside it for us for a new year. But, regardless of the final verdict, one thing is certain. By observing this Day of Atonement properly, that is, by doing our duty to God, we will be doing our duty to man and thus hastening the day when all men will behave toward each other as children of God and build a world where all may live happily and peacefully. Remember this vital lesson as you observe these sacred "Solemn Days."

HOW THE HIGH HOLY DAYS ARE OBSERVED

In the previous sections we have seen that the High Holy Days are serious festivals because of our deep concern about our fate in the coming year. Now we will try to answer the questions: How do we show our seriousness during this Holy Day period? What do we do to make this period different from other times of the year?

To put it briefly, we spend more time in the synagogue than usual because of lengthier services, and we sound the shofar at various times during these holy days. Each of these observances will be further explained very shortly.

But, as a matter of fact, the preparations for the High Holy Days actually begin at least a full month before their arrival. Commencing with the month of Elul (the month preceding Tishri, when Rosh HaShana is observed) the shofar is sounded every weekday morning at the close of the services, to make us aware of the approach of these High Holy Days.

Then, on the Saturday night before Rosh HaShana, beginning shortly after midnight, we begin reciting special prayers called *S'lihot* (forgiveness) and continue until Rosh HaShana. After Rosh HaShana they are resumed and continued through Yom Kippur. (These S'lihot prayers are also recited on certain other days of the year.)

Still another feature of the High Holy Days is the special chant used for the prayers. These melodies are much more tuneful and elaborate than those used for other prayers throughout the year.

THE HOW OF ROSH HASHANA

We Jews regard Rosh HaShana as the "New Year." It is our New Year but not to be confused with the New Year celebration on the first of January. There are a number of differences between the two. One of the most significant is perhaps best understood from the greetings used for each. Whereas for January first the greeting is "Happy New Year," for Rosh HaShana it is *L'Shanah Tovah Tikateyvu!* (May you be inscribed in the Book of Life for a good year). When we extend such greeting to one another we are being reminded that our Rosh HaShana is the "Day of Judgment." In this way we help spread the message of this solemn festival. The words *L'Shanah Tovah* are also found on every greeting card which Jews customarily send one another. In fact, they are known as "L'Shanah Tovah cards."

Since Rosh HaShana is known in the Bible only as the "Day of Sounding the Shofar" this ceremony naturally plays a most important part in the synagogue service. The shofar is sounded on both days of the Rosh HaShana services, unless one of them is the Sabbath, when shofar blowing is forbidden. All Jews, men and women, young and old, are required to hear the shofar sounded.

The shofar service begins shortly after the reading of the Torah when the first series of the total one hundred notes is sounded. Certain specific prayers are recited during this service. The man who blows the shofar is known as a "Baal Tokeah." The three different calls of the shofar are:

T'KIAH   (one long blast)
SH'VARIM (three broken blasts)
T'RUAH   (nine quick staccato notes)

As the Rabbi calls out each of these words in turn, that particular call is sounded. Then, during the *Mussaf* (Additional) service, another series of calls is sounded in a similar manner. The final series of shofar calls takes place toward the close of the Mussaf service.

As has already been mentioned the High Holy Days are primarily synagogue-centered festivals. The services are, therefore, longer than usual. However, even though special prayers are inserted into every service (evening, morning and afternoon) it is the Mussaf which is the longest, especially because of its major divisions. These are called *Malchiot* (Royalty), which tells of God as King; *Zichronot* (Remembering), where the events that God remembers on Rosh HaShana are mentioned; and *Shofrot* (Sounding of the Shofar), which recall events connected with the shofar.

A few additional features of the Mussaf service include the following:

1) When the *Aleynu* prayer is recited (during the Malchiot) the cantor and the congregation kneel, as a reminder of the Temple days. (Now, Jews are forbidden to kneel except on the High Holy Days.)

2) The *Unetaneh Tokef* prayer is also recited during the Malchiot portion. This prayer is said to have been written by Rabbi Amnon of Mayence during the Middle Ages. (See some of the reference books on Rosh HaShana for details of this moving story.) In this prayer God is pictured as a shepherd counting and judging His flocks. This prayer is also said on Yom Kippur.

Another special Rosh HaShana ceremony is the *Tashlich* service. During the late afternoon of the first day of Rosh HaShana it is customary to go to the bank of a river or any other flowing body of water where fish are found. Special prayers are recited and each person then shakes out the corners of his garments in order to show that he is casting his sins into the water in an effort to correct his ways.

Since Rosh HaShana is more a synagogue than a home festival there are not many special ceremonies for the home. However, we do observe the following:

On Rosh HaShana Eve the candle-lighting and Kiddush before the meal are much the same as on every festival. But the Hallas (Sabbath and festival loaves) are round instead of the usual long shaped to symbolize the hope for an all around good year.

Then, on the second night, it is customary to taste a new fruit (one not yet tasted that year) and to pronounce the *Shehecheyanu* blessing thanking God for having allowed us to eat this new fruit.

Observance of the ceremony of Kapparot.

We see therefore that the Jew looks upon his new year seriously. For him it is not an occasion of gaiety and merriment, nor, on the other hand, one of sadness and gloom. Instead, Rosh HaShana is the time for deep thought and careful consideration both of the year just passed and the one just beginning. The Jew faces the new year with joy and faith in God and the hope that He will answer our prayers because He is a just and loving God.

During the Ten Days of Penitence (between Rosh HaShana and Yom Kippur) we try to improve our conduct, hoping that if a favorable verdict has not yet been inscribed for us in the Book of Life, our last-minute efforts to improve may influence God to change it for a better one.

The day following Rosh HaShana is a minor fast-day called *Tzom Gedaliah* (The Fast of Gedaliah) in memory of Gedaliah, a popular Jewish Governor of Israel who was killed after the Babylonians had destroyed the First Temple. This day was designated as a day of fasting because of the Jews' deep sorrow for their lost hopes of rebuilding their nation.

The Sabbath between Rosh HaShana and Yom Kippur is known as *Shabbat Shuva* (The Sabbath of Repentance). It bears this name because the opening word of the Haftorah of this Sabbath is *Shuva*. That afternoon it is customary for the Rabbi to deliver a special sermon on a learned subject dealing with the High Holy Days.

The special greeting for the days between Rosh HaShana through Yom Kippur is *G'mar Hatimah Tovah* (May your final verdict be a good one!).

HOW YOM KIPPUR IS OBSERVED

The preparations for Yom Kippur begin on the previous day, which is called *Erev Yom Kippur*. This is a half-holiday and several observances are connected with it.

First, as on the days immediately preceding it, it is customary on Erev Yom Kippur to ask forgiveness of one another, that is, for the sins between man and man. (See the WHY of Yom Kippur in this chapter.) Then on the night before Erev Yom Kippur, we observe the ceremony of *Kapparot*.

In this ceremony, a few prayers are recited and a rooster is offered for a Jew or a hen for a Jewess, in the hope that the fowl thus offered will serve as a substitute for us as we ask forgiveness for our sins. Nowadays, however, money donated to charity may be used in place of the fowl. This ceremony (which consists of swinging the fowl over our heads as we say the prayers) recalls the ancient sin-offering in the Temple of old.

Then comes the fasting-meal, which is served before sunset. Inasmuch as fasting on Erev Yom Kippur is forbidden, we must eat heartily of this final meal before the fast begins. During the Yom Kippur fast, which lasts from evening to evening, no food or drink whatsoever may be tasted.

Who must fast? Every Jewish man and women, aged thirteen or more, is required to fast on Yom Kippur. However, anyone too sick or too weak physically is excused from fasting. Also, children under thirteen are not required to fast. But even young children can show their desire to fast and to observe Yom Kippur in the following ways. First, as a child approaches the age of thirteen, he should delay his meal-time on Yom Kippur as long as possible. Then, regardless of a child's age, he can be made conscious of the holiness of this day by refraining from eating such unnecessary foods as candy, ice cream and the like.

After the fasting-meal and just before leaving for the synagogue, the father of the house blesses his children.

In the synagogue the Yom Kippur service begins while there is still day light. This is known as the *Kol Nidre* service. The words "Kol Nidre" are the first in a famous prayer which is chanted only by the cantor and choir. In this prayer we ask that all oaths and vows that we took but did not intend to fulfill, be considered null and void, as though they were never spoken. The cantor (with the aid of a choir) thus becomes the congregation's spokesman before God. During this Kol Nidre service all the Torah scrolls are taken from the ark and held by some of the most respected members of the congregation.

During the High Holidays it is customary for the cantor and the men of the congregation to wear a white gown known as a *kittel*.

In the course of the evening service that follows, the confession prayers are recited. As we say the *Al Heyt* (these are the opening words of every line of this prayer) we beat our breasts as a reminder that our heart has led us into sin. Because we confess only once a year, and do so as a group (not each person separately), we mention all the *kinds* of sins we might have committed, and finally, we confess directly to God and not to any one person.

But, you may ask, why confess a sin if you have not committed it? We do this because we all feel responsible to one another. That is, any

Jew's sins are the concern of *every* Jew. This, then, is what confession means in Judaism; it is another sign of the unity of the Jewish people. This same confession prayer is recited during the remaining services of Yom Kippur as well.

One important feature of the Mussaf (additional) service is the *Avodah*. The prayers recited here describe the solemn Yom Kippur services in the days of the ancient Temple in Jerusalem. During this service it is customary to kneel three times, as was done in the Temple. (For a fuller description of this and other Yom Kippur ceremonies, read Edidin, pp. 62-68.)

In the *Minha* (afternoon) service, the Haftorah reading (from the Books of the Prophets) consists of reading the entire book of Jonah (the story of Jonah and the whale). The privilege of reciting this famous haftorah is considered one of the highest honors to be had in the synagogue.

The final and closing service of Yom Kippur is called the *Neilah* service. During Neilah we feel that just as the gates of prayer are about to close, we make our final plea to God to hear our prayers, to forgive our sins, and to give us life for the coming year. The ark remains open, but only for true and sincere prayers. Every one who can do it, remains standing during this entire service.

At the close of Neilah, one long blast of the shofar is sounded after which we say *L'Shanah ha-ba'ah Bee-rushalaim!* ("Next year may we all be in Jerusalem!") This is the sign that Yom Kippur is officially over. Thus we see that, as the High Holy Days are ushered in with the sound of the shofar, so they end with the shofar sound.

During the long Yom Kippur day (the only time in the year that we will spend an entire day in the synagogue) the many prayers and ceremonies will be better understood and appreciated if we know something about them. That has been our purpose. If you review all this material just before Yom Kippur and keep it in mind as you follow the service, they will take on a new meaning and hold a greater interest for you. You will also come closer to the deeper meaning of repentance, which says, "I am truly sorry for my misdeeds. Let me now try to do better." This will give you hope for bettering yourself in every way. Therefore, remember these lessons of the High Holy Days not just for ten days, but for 365 days of every year.

G'MAR HATIMAH TOVAH!
(MAY YOUR FINAL VERDICT BE A FAVORABLE ONE!)

HIGH HOLY DAYS TERMS

AL HEYT	The opening words of the Yom Kippur confession prayer
ASERET Y'MEY T'SHUVAH	The Ten Days of Penitence
AVODAH	The prayer recited during the Mussaf (additional) service of Yom Kippur. It reminds us of Temple days
BAAL TOKEAH	The man who sounds the Shofar
ELUL	The Hebrew month before Rosh HaShana
G'MAR HATIMAH TOVAH	"May your final verdict be a favorable one"—the greeting for the days after Rosh HaShana
HIGH HOLY DAYS	Rosh HaShana and Yom Kippur
KAPPAROT	A special ceremony performed the day before Yom Kippur, when a rooster, hen or money is used
KOL NIDRE	The special service which is recited just before the evening service of Yom Kippur
L'SHANAH HA-BA'AH BEE-RUSHALAIM	"Next Year in Jerusalem"—the final words of the Yom Kippur service
L'SHANAH TOVAH TIKATEYVU	"May you be inscribed for a Good Year"—the greeting for Rosh HaShana
MACHZOR	A festival prayerbook
MALCHIOT	"Royalty"—the first of the three divisions of the Mussaf service for Rosh HaShana
MUSSAF	The special additional service for Sabbath and all festivals
NEILAH	The closing service of Yom Kippur
ROSH HASHANA	"Head of the Year"

SHABBAT SHUVA	The Sabbath between Rosh HaShana and Yom Kippur
SHOFAR	A ram's horn blown on Rosh HaShana (and at the end of Yom Kippur)
SHOFROT	"Sounding of the Shofar"—the third of the three divisions of the Rosh HaShana Mussaf service
SH'VARIM	3 broken blasts, the 2nd of the shofar calls
S'LIHOT	Prayers of forgiveness which are recited during the High Holy Days
TASHLICH	A Rosh HaShana afternoon service, which takes place beside a flowing stream or river
TEN DAYS OF PENITENCE	The ten-day period which includes the days from Rosh HaShana through Yom Kippur
TISHRI	The seventh month of the Hebrew year when the High Holy Days come
T'KIAH	One of the shofar calls, consisting of one long blast
T'RUAH	The third of the shofar calls which consists of nine quick staccato notes
TZOM G'DALIAH	The Fast of Gedaliah, which comes on the day after Rosh HaShana
UNETANEH TOKEF	The name of a well-known High Holy Day prayer
YOM HA-DIN	"Day of Judgment," a name for Rosh HaShana
YOM HA-ZIKARON	"Day of Remembrance," a name for Rosh HaShana
YOM KIPPUR	"Day of Atonement" (forgiveness)
YOM T'RUAH	"Day of Sounding the Shofar," the name for Rosh HaShana as given in the Torah
ZICHRONOT	"Remembering"—the 2nd of the 3 divisions of the Rosh HaShana Mussaf service

NUMBERS TO REMEMBER FOR HIGH HOLY DAYS

1   Rosh HaShana begins on the *first* day of Tishri, it is also the *first* day of the new year. Yom Kippur lasts but *one* day

2   *Two* days of Rosh HaShana are observed

3   There are *three* kinds of shofar calls, and
    three divisions of the Mussaf service for Rosh HaShana

5   On Yom Kippur *five* services are held

6   On Yom Kippur *six* men are called to the Torah

7   Tishri (when the High Holy Days come) is the *seventh* month of the year
    There are *seven* days between Rosh HaShana and Yom Kippur

10 We observe *ten* days of penitence
    Yom Kippur falls on the *tenth* day of the month of Tishri

100 Every Jew must hear a total of *100* calls of the shofar on Rosh HaShana

QUIZ QUESTIONS FOR ROSH HASHANA

QUESTIONS:

1. The name "Rosh HaShana" means
2. Give 3 other names for Rosh Ha-Shana and the meaning of each.

3. The Hebrew date of Rosh Ha-Shana is:
4. Which are the High Holy Days?
5. a) The Hebrew term for the High Holy Days is————.
   b) What does it mean?
6. What is a shofar?

7. a) When is the shofar blown?
   b) When is it forbidden to be blown?
   c) Who must hear it blown?

8. The shofar reminds us of two important events in Jewish history. Name them.

9. What is meant by a *Baal Tokeah*?
10. Every Jew must hear a total of—— calls on Rosh Hashana.
11. a) There are how many different kinds of calls of the shofar?
    b) Name and describe each one.

ANSWERS:

1. Head of the year
2. a) Yom Ha-Zikaron: Day of Remembering
   b) Yom Ha Din: Day of Judgment
   c) Yom T'ruah: Day of Sounding the Shofar
3. 1st and 2nd of Tishri
4. Rosh HaShana and Yom Kippur
5. a) Yamim Noraim
   b) Days of Awe (Fear)

6. A ram's horn that is blown on Rosh HaShana
7. a) On Rosh Hashana, during the morning services and at the end of Yom Kippur day
   b) When Rosh HaShana falls on a Sabbath
   c) Every Jew, young and old

8. a) When Abraham attempted to sacrifice his own son Isaac
   b) Before and after the Ten Commandments were given
9. The person who blows the shofar
10. One hundred
11. a) Three
    b) T'kiah—One long blast
       Sh'varim—3 broken blasts
       T'ruah—9 staccato blasts or notes

12. Name the 3 parts of the Mussaf (Additional) service for Rosh HaShana.

12. a) Malchiot (Royalty)
    b) Zichronot (Remembrance or Remembering)
    c) Shofrot (Sounding of the shofar)

13. What synagogue ceremony is observed on the High Holy Days but is forbidden at any other time?

13. Kneeling during certain prayers

14. During Rosh HaShana and Yom Kippur services the cantor and others kneel. Why?

14. As a reminder of this practice which was followed in the Temple

15. Who wrote the prayer *Unetaneh Tokef*?

15. Rabbi Amnon of Mayence

16. When is the *Unetaneh Tokef* prayer recited?

16. During the Mussaf services of Rosh HaShana and Yom Kippur

17. *Tashlich* is ————.

17. A special ceremony of the first afternoon of Rosh HaShana when special prayers are recited beside the banks of a stream or a river

18. What color is used in the synagogue on the High Holy Days?

18. White

19. a) The Hebrew greeting for Rosh HaShana is ——————.
    b) Give its meaning.

19. a) L'Shanah Tovah Tikateyvu
    b) May you be written down for a good year

20. Name two special foods used on Rosh HaShana.

20. Apple and honey

21. What is the shape of the *Hallas* used for Rosh HaShana?

21. Round (instead of the usual long oval shaped)

22. What table custom is observed on the 2nd night of Rosh HaShana?

22. Eating a new fruit for the first time in the year

23. What do we ask God in our prayers on Rosh HaShana?

23. That He give us a year of life and a chance to turn over a new leaf that year

24. When, before Rosh HaShana, do we begin blowing the shofar?

24. During the entire month of Elul at the close of each weekday morning service

25. For the Jew, the most important meaning of Rosh HaShana is:
    a) It is our New Year
    b) A time for examining our conduct
    c) Forgiveness of sins

26. In the Torah, Rosh HaShana is called:
    a) Day of Judgment
    b) Day of Remembrance
    c) Day of Sounding the Shofar

25. b) Examining our conduct

26. c) Day of Sounding the Shofar

QUIZ QUESTIONS FOR YOM KIPPUR

QUESTIONS:

1. What do the words Yom Kippur mean?
2. Give the Hebrew date of Yom Kippur
3. In which of the following customs does Yom Kippur differ from Rosh HaShana? Fasting, praying, reading the Torah or kneeling?
4. I am a prayer that is recited just before Yom Kippur. Name me.
5. Why is the Kol Nidre Prayer recited by the cantor only?
6. What is said in the Kol Nidre prayer?
7. For what important thing do we ask in most of the Yom Kippur prayers?
8. Who must confess sins on Yom Kippur?
9. What kinds of sins are confessed in the *Viduy* prayers?
10. Why must a Jew who thinks he never sinned at all, nevertheless confess sins?
11. a) What is the *Avodah*?
    b) Where does it belong on Yom Kippur?

ANSWERS:

1. Day of Atonement or forgiveness
2. 10th of Tishri
3. Fasting
4. Kol Nidre
5. Because he acts as the spokesman before God for the entire congregation
6. All vows and oaths which any Jew took without meaning what he said are to be considered as though they had never been said
7. That our sins be forgiven
8. Every Jew
9. Those which any person might commit during the year
10. Because we all feel responsible for one another's conduct
11. a) A Prayer which describes the ancient Temple service on Yom Kippur
    b) In the Mussaf (Additional) service

12. I am a famous book of the prophets read on Yom Kippur. Name me.

12. Book of Jonah

13. What types of sins are forgiven by God on Yom Kippur?

13. Those between man and God

14. What must be done for a sin committed against a fellow man to be forgiven?

14. We must ask that person himself to forgive that sin

15. Who must fast on Yom Kippur?

15. Every Jew 13 years of age or over

16. There are ——— services on Yom Kippur. Name them in correct order.

16. Five: Maariv (Evening), Shacharit (Morning), Mussaf (Additional), Minha (Afternoon), Neilah (Closing)

17. Why is Yom Kippur the holiest day of the year?

17. On that day the Book of Life is sealed

18. What special custom is observed during the entire Neilah service?

18. The ark remains open during the entire service

19. Which ceremony tells us that Yom Kippur is over?

19. One long blast of the shofar

20. Name the most important duty which the High Priest used to perform on Yom Kippur.

20. Enter the Holy of Holies

21. What words are recited after the shofar is sounded on Yom Kippur?

21. L'Shanah ha-ba'ah Bee-rushalaim (Next year in Jerusalem)

22. Give the special greetings for Yom Kippur.

22. G'mar Hatimah Tovah (May your final verdict be a favorable one)

23. What does the father of the house do just before leaving for the synagogue on Yom Kippur Eve?

23. Blesses his wife and children

24. What should a child, under 13, do about fasting on Yom Kippur?

24. a) Delay his meal time
    b) Avoid eating unnecessary foods such as candy, ice cream, etc.

SUKKOT

When a Rabbi once asked a little boy, "Why don't you want to go to the synagogue?" the youngster replied: "Why should I? Every time I go there, all they do is cry. I don't want to cry. I want to be happy and have fun."

"Have you ever been there on Sukkot?" asked the Rabbi.

"No, only on big holidays. But what is Sukkot?" asked the lad, full of curiosity. The Rabbi then told all about this happy holiday.

If you have ever felt this way about going to the synagogue, you have many pleasant things to learn.

You may have seen Sukkot being observed. Perhaps you've seen a *sukka*, maybe also an *ethrog* and *lulav*. They are part of HOW we observe the festival of Sukkot. But you may not know WHY we do these things on Sukkot or why we placed the WHY portion before the HOW in our explanations. Since on the Sukkot festival we use many objects of interest (such as the ethrog and lulav) you will satisfy your curiosity by discovering what they are used for and what they mean.

Another thing: did you know that on Sukkot we are instructed to be *only happy?* That is what our Torah tells us. Therefore, as you read through the WHY section you will find out what it is that makes Sukkot such a festival of real joy.

The HOW shows many ways of enjoying that happiness. As you enjoy these, you will also learn a bit more about our people and you will see that the Jew naturally tends to be happy. Whenever he isn't, it is usually not for long.

"For Further Reading" lists books in which you will find suggestions for art and handiwork, and a variety of other material. The "Terms" and "Numbers" will be of great help in remembering this material.

HAPPY SUKKOT!

THE WHY OF SUKKOT

Following the High Holidays we now come to the happiest and gayest of all the festivals in our calendar. This is the Sukkot Festival, which is actually a few festivals combined into one. First come the seven days of Sukkot (15-21 of the month of Tishri) and then, *Sh'mini Atzeret* and *Simhat Torah* (22-23 of Tishri). Each of these will be explained in greater detail.

But Sukkot differs from most of the other festivals in that it does not celebrate any one event or joyful occasion of the year. In other words, we observe Sukkot not because something special happened during these days, but rather because this is the time of the year when we are commanded to be happy and gay.

Sukkot, as you may remember, is one of the *Shalosh Regalim* (the three pilgrimage festivals) when the Israelites were commanded in the Torah to make a pilgrimage (a journey to the Temple) in Jerusalem and bring their offerings. But of these three (Passover, Shavuot and Sukkot) the third was the happiest. What made it such a gay holiday?

First, Sukkot marked the end of the fruit harvest, when the Israelites brought their fruit offerings to the Temple as a sign of thanksgiving for God's kindness and goodness. This was the jolliest season of the year because the Jew rejoiced then not only over his fruit harvest but over his produce during the entire year.

But his joy was accompanied by memories. The Israelites were urged always to remember their forty years of wandering in the desert after leaving Egypt. During those years, when they had to keep moving from place to place, they could not build a strong, permanent home. Instead, they had to live in a small, frail hut called a *sukka*. This sukka gave them little protection from winds, storms and wild animals, etc. But God protected them all those days even though nothing stronger than a sukka was their home. That is why we commemorate this event by using a sukka for seven days. How the sukka is to be used is told in the HOW section which follows.

There are various other names for this Sukkot festival and they suggest other reasons for its observance.

Sukkot seems to have been the very earliest of all the festivals, because in both the Bible and in post-Biblical literature it is often referred to merely as *Hag* (The Festival). (See Leviticus, 23:39-40.) This shows that it must have been both the earliest and the most important of the festivals.

However, a fuller indication of Sukkot as a joyous holiday is found in the name *Z'man Simhateynu* (The Season of our Rejoicing). What was the occasion for all this joy? Their thanksgiving to God for the bountiful harvest. That is also the reason for its being called *Hag Ha-Asif* (The Festival of Ingathering) as well.

During the days of the Temple the Israelites would bring their fruit-harvest offerings to the Temple in Jerusalem where they would express their joy to the fullest. Examples are given in the HOW portion.

Today, however, the only reminders we have of those days are the "Four Species." These consist of the *ethrog* (a citron), a *lulav* (palm branch) and, attached to the lulav, the two sets of leaves—*hadassim* (myrtles, which are short and round) and *aravot* (willows, long and narrow). The Bible commands us (Leviticus, 23:40) to use these Four Species during the seven days of Sukkot.

Various explanations have been given for this but perhaps the best known is the following: The ethrog represents the heart; the lulav—the spine; the myrtles—the eyes; and the willows—the lips or mouth.

The most popular name for this festival is, of course, *Hag Ha-Sukkot* (The Festival of Booths or Tabernacles). This name refers to the commandment (Leviticus, 23: 42-43) to dwell in booths for seven days.

However, the sukka is not only a reminder of our past history, but also a symbol of hospitality. From your reading of Jewish history you will remember that throughout the ages the Jew has always been known for his hospitality and friendship, even toward strangers. This quality is emphasized on Sukkot.

Following the first two days of Sukkot (which are major holidays, when no work is permitted), come four days of *Hol-Ha-Moed* (the half-holiday). Ordinary work is permitted during these days, but the festival spirit still prevails and many of the observances of the first two days still apply.

Then comes *Hoshana Rabba*, the seventh day. Even though most work is permitted even on this day, it is a bit more significant than the preceding four days. *Hoshana Rabba* gets its name from the *Hoshana* prayer which is recited on Sukkot. More of this will be found in the HOW portion.

The last two days of the Sukkot Festival are known as *Sh'mini Atzeret* and *Simhat Torah*. They are separate festivals, in a way, but are considered to be part of Sukkot because they follow the latter immediately. Both these days are also observed as major festivals.

Sh'mini Atzeret (which means the eighth day of solemn assembly) is the only solemn day of the nine: first, because we then recite the prayer for rain in Israel; and, secondly, because of the Yizkor (memorial for the departed) which is said towards the end of every festival.

However, Sh'mini Atzeret is not a sad day, but only a bit more solemn than the previous seven.

Simhat Torah is the last. Here we have one of the gayest and merriest of all our festivals. What is the source of joy on this day? Why, the Torah! You see, since the Torah is Life itself for the Jew it is but natural that it should also bring him great pleasure each time he reads it through to the end. That is really something to celebrate.

As you may know, the Torah is read in the synagogue every Sabbath; a specific portion (called a *Sedra*) is set aside for each week. This reading continues week after week until we come to the very last sedra. This portion is reserved for Simhat Torah, which thus marks the completion of the yearly cycle of Torah reading.

But concluding the Torah reading is only one half of the celebration. The other half consists of *beginning* the reading of the Torah all over again from its very first word. In this way Torah reading never ends, because no sooner do we finish, than we start all over again. This too is discussed in the HOW section which tells how to express our happiness in a truly Jewish manner.

From the foregoing you can see that the Jew's source of happiness is something that is lasting and permanent and not something that exists for but a moment. It is a kind of happiness that makes you look forward to the return of Sukkot because it leaves you not only happy but also proud of being a Jew.

Ethrog box, Holland, 19th Century.

HOW SUKKOT IS OBSERVED

Most of the Sukkot observances practiced are the same ones which were part of the Temple services of old. First and foremost is the sukka, which gives this festival its best-known name. However, even though the commandment of dwelling in a sukka for seven days is found in the Torah, nothing is said about its construction. It was only later that the Rabbis of the Talmud composed a clear and definite set of laws to guide us in this matter.

Although a sukka may be constructed of almost any kind of material, there is one strict rule that must be followed: it must not have a roof. Instead, its top must consist of slats upon which fresh green branches (called *S'chach*) must be laid in such a manner that the sukka will have more shade than light and that the stars may be seen through the leaves.

Every time we enter the sukka, special prayers and blessings must be pronounced as well as when we leave it for the last time. All meals must be eaten in the sukka, except when weather conditions prevent this. It is also customary to invite guests into the sukka. In fact, one of the prayers (called *oshpizin*) mentions this fact. It is also considered a mitzvah to decorate the sukka, something the children often take pride in doing well.

These, then, are but a few ways in which we use the sukka during the seven days. And if we should feel any discomfort in the sukka, it serves to remind us of the Israelites' forty hard years of wandering in the desert.

At the Western Wall on Sukkot.

The Four Species (the ethrog, lulav, myrtles and willows) are reminders of the late harvest offerings of the Israelites during Temple days. The ethrog (the citron) must be in perfect condition, without any defects, to be approved for use. In fact, the ethrog is the most important of these Four Species. After Sukkot, it may be prepared for food.

The lulav (palm branch) must be green and fresh and also in good condition. The leaves (the myrtles and willows) which are tied to the lulav, must also be fresh and green, although they may be replaced if they become withered.

When the blessings over the Four Species are recited, the lulav in the right hand, and the ethrog in the left hand, are held close to each other to show that the Four Species are united as one. These blessings are said every morning of the seven days, except on the Sabbath, when the ethrog and lulav are not to be used, or even touched.

Every morning of the seven days, when the prayer called *Hoshana* is recited, those who have an ethrog and lulav march around the synagogue in a procession. This ceremony is another reminder of Temple days.

During the Hallel prayer, it is customary to shake the lulav during certain parts of the prayer, in six different directions: To the North, to the South, to the East, and to the West, up towards heaven and down to the earth.

Celebrating Sukkot in Jerusalem. This Bucharian Jew also uses his sukka for study while his grandchild looks on.

While the Temple was still standing one of the most popular ceremonies was the *Simhat Bet Ha-Shoevah* (the water-pouring festival). On the second night of Sukkot, a huge parade was formed which led into the Temple. It was followed by a very colorful and impressive celebration. Some synagogues and organizations still observe this custom today, as another reminder of ancient days.

Even though work is permitted during *Hol Ha-Moed* (the four days of half-holiday after the first two) we still do only that work which is absolutely necessary, because the festival spirit is still in force. In fact, most of the prayers of the first two days are also recited during Hol Ha-Moed.

The seventh day of Sukkot, known as *Hoshana Rabba*, is a bit more solemn than the preceding four and some of the Sabbath and festival prayers are said on this day.

Now, as noted above, on each day of Sukkot, a special Hoshana prayer is recited as the congregation marches around the synagogue. But on Hoshana Rabba, all of the previous Hoshanas are recited with the addition of a number of others. The procession now circles seven times around with each person carrying his own ethrog and lulav.

The seven days of Sukkot officially end on Hoshana Rabba. But the two days immediately following, *Sh'mini Atzeret* and *Simhat Torah*, are also observed as major festivals. Because Sh'mini Atzeret is more solemn than all the other days of the Sukkot Festivals, the prayer for rain (in Israel) is recited. The cantor, wearing a white robe (called a *kittel*) as on the High Holidays, chants the prayer as he does on the High Holidays. Also, the *Yizkor*, the memorial prayer for the dead, is said.

On Sh'mini Atzeret, however, all other festival observances continue, such as holiday food and clothes, a festive atmosphere in the home, etc.

But, when Simhat Torah comes on the next day, there is no limit to our fun and gaiety, because of our extreme joy over the Torah. First, during the evening service, all the Torah scrolls are taken from the Ark. Each is given to one man selected for the honor of carrying it in a procession around the synagogue. This march is called a *Hakafah*. The man at the head of the procession chants a special prayer as he marches, the Torah scroll clasped in his arms.

As the hakafot continue seven times around, as many men as possible are honored with a hakafah. (Often boys too are thus honored.) As the men march around carrying the scrolls, the children follow behind them carrying flags on the tip of which an apple is stuck (and sometimes even a lighted candle inside the apple). Some children even carry miniature Torah scrolls.

Following the seven hakafot all but one of the Torah scrolls are returned to the Ark. Three men are then called up as the Torah portion for the evening is read.

Incidentally, this is the only time during the entire year when the Torah is read during the evening.

During the entire evening there is excited singing and dancing and other forms of merriment.

The following morning, beginning with the Torah reading, the same procedure continues. However, a few additions are made, especially since on Simhat Torah the aim is to give every man present an aliyah (honor of being called up to the Torah). Therefore, each time a portion is read, not one but several men are called up at once. This continues until every man has had his aliyah.

Even the smaller boys, below the age of thirteen, are called up for an aliyah on Simhat Torah. This custom is called *Kol Ha-n'arim* (all the boys). As the lads stand on the platform beside the Torah, a large Talit held up by four men is spread over them and they all recite the Torah blessings together.

But the two highest honors to be had on Simhat Torah are called *Hattan Torah* and *Hattan B'reshit*. The Hattan Torah has the honor of calling up to the Torah all those who will read the very last words of the Torah, while the Hattan B'reshit similarly calls up those who are to begin the Torah reading again with the opening words of Genesis.

As you can see, we have here the kind of joy and pleasure that are truly meaningful and lasting. The joy over the Torah has always been a very bright spot in the life of the Jew.

The best proof of this is our Jewish history. For hundreds of years the Jews suffered and were persecuted in many lands. Life was very bitter for them. But the joy they derived from festivals such as Sukkot and Simhat Torah boosted their morale, never allowing them to give up hope. They appreciated this joy and were closely attached to the Torah and its way of life.

To us too the Torah says "And you shall rejoice on your festival (Sukkot) and you shall be nothing but happy". So be sure to fulfill those instructions!

HAG SA-ME-ACH! HAPPY SUKKOT TO ALL OF YOU!

TERMS FOR THE SUKKOT FESTIVALS

ALIYAH	The honor of being called to the Torah
ARAVOT	The long, narrow willow leaves that are attached to the lulav
ETHROG	A citron, one of the Four Species used during Sukkot
THE FOUR SPECIES	The ethrog, lulav, aravot and hadassim
HADASSIM	The short, round myrtle leaves that are attached to the lulav
HAG	"The Festival"—a name for Sukkot in rabbinic literature
HAG HA-ASIF	"Feast of Ingathering"—a name for Sukkot
HAG HA-SUKKOT	"Feast of the Booths"—another name for Sukkot
HAG SA-ME-ACH	"Happy Holiday"!—Sukkot greeting
HAKAFOT	The honor of marching around with a Torah scroll on Simhat Torah
HATTAN B'RESHIT	The special honor of being called up on Simhat Torah for the very beginning of the reading of the Torah
HATTAN TORAH	The special Simhat Torah honor of being called up for the very last reading of the Torah
HOL HA-MOED	The "half-holiday"—that portion of the festival when work is permitted; the four middle days
HOSHANOT	Prayers that are said on every day of Sukkot
HOSHANA RABBA	The name given to the 7th day of Sukkot
KITTEL	A white robe worn by the cantor on certain days of a festival and on the High Holidays
KOL HA-N'ARIM	"All the boys"—the special Simhat Torah ceremony of having all pre-Bar Mitzvah boys recite the Torah blessings together
LULAV	A palm branch—One of the "Four Species"
OSHPIZIN	"Guests"—a prayer that is said before entering the sukka

S'CHACH	The green covering of the sukka
SEDRA	The weekly Torah portion that is read on each Sabbath
SHALOSH REGALIM	"The Three Festivals of Rejoicing": *Pesah*, *Shavuot* and *Sukkot*
SH'MINI ATZERET	"Eighth Day of Solemn Assembly"—the name for the 8th Day of the Sukkot festival
SIMHAT BET HA-SHOEVAH	"The Water-Pouring Festival" that used to be observed during the days of the Temple
SIMHAT TORAH	The very last of the Sukkot festivals, when a gay Torah celebration takes place in the synagogue
SUKKA	A small hut used during Sukkot
SUKKOT	The name of this festival
TABERNACLES	An English name for Sukkot
TALMUD	The Oral Law, which follows and explains the Written Law, the Torah
T'FILAT GESHEM	The prayer for rain, recited on Sh'mini Atzeret
TISHRI	The Hebrew month in which Sukkot comes
YIZKOR	The memorial prayer for the dead, which is recited on or near the last day of every major festival
Z'MAN SIMHATEYNU	"The Season of our Rejoicing," another name for Sukkot

NUMBERS TO REMEMBER FOR THE SUKKOT FESTIVALS

- 2   The first *two* days of Sukkot
- 3   The *Three* Festivals of Rejoicing
- 4   The *Four* Species
     The *four* days of Hol Ha-Moed
- 5   The Torah consists of the *Five* Books of Moses

7   The *seven* days of Sukkot
    Hoshana Rabba is on the *seventh* day of Sukkot
    Seven times around on Simhat Torah

8   Sh'mini Atzeret is the *eighth* day of Solemn Assembly

9   The *nine* days of the Sukkot festivals

15 Sukkot begins on the *15th* day of Tishri

40 The Israelites wandered in the desert for *forty* years

*Examining an ethrog in Mea Shearim, Jerusalem.
(Courtesy Keren Hayesod.)*

QUIZ QUESTIONS FOR THE SUKKOT FESTIVALS

QUESTIONS   *ANSWERS*

1. What is the meaning of the word Sukkot?
2. Give the opening Hebrew date of "Sukkot."
3. a) What is meant by Hol Ha-Moed?
   b) For how many days is it observed during Sukkot?
   c) How does it differ from the first two days of Sukkot?
4. I am a little hut with fresh greens for a roof. Give my Hebrew name.
5. What is meant by S'chach?
6. How does a sukka differ from any other hut or booth?
7. In what special way must the top of the sukka be arranged?
8. Why do we live in a sukka during Sukkot?
9. For how many days do we use a sukka during Sukkot?
10. The last day the sukka is occupied is called ———.
11. a) Four objects used on Sukkot are called by what common names?
    b) Name the four objects.
12. Describe the ethrog and lulav.

1. Booths, or huts
2. 15th of Tishri
3. a) Half-holiday
   b) Four
   c) Work is permitted
4. Sukka
5. The fresh green covering of the sukka
6. It has no solid roof, but is covered with S'chach
7. The branches must be so arranged that there is more shade than light
8. To remind us of how the Israelites lived in booths for 40 years
9. Seven
10. Hoshana Rabba, the Seventh Day
11. a) Arbat Ha-Minim ("The Four Species")
    b) The ethrog, lulav, aravot and hadassim
12. Ethrog—a citrus, lemon-like fruit
    Lulav—a tall palm branch

13. We are ethrog and lulav.
    a) Which of us has some taste?
    b) Which has a pleasant odor?
    c) Which would you call handsome looking?

14. Two sets of leaves are attached to the lulav.
    a) Name them and describe them.
    b) Give the Hebrew name of each.

15. a) What is meant by "Hoshanot"?
    b) How did it get this name?

16. Which day of Sukkot is called "Hoshana Rabba"?

17. How does Sukkot remind us of the agricultural life of our people?

18. I am Sukkot, one of the Three Festivals. Name my other companions.

19. On which days of Sukkot are the Hoshanot recited?

20. By what other names am I, Sukkot, called?

21. How does Hoshana Rabba gets its name?

22. I am the "Simhat Bet Ha-Shoevah."
    a) Give my English name.
    b) During which period of our history was I observed?

---

13. a) Ethrog
    b) Ethrog
    c) Lulav

14. a) Willows — long, narrow leaves
       Myrtles — short, round leaves
    b) Willows — Aravot
       Myrtles — Hadassim

15. a) Marching around the synagogue holding the ethrog and lulav
    b) From the first two words of a prayer recited during the procession. They mean: Please Save Us!

16. The seventh day

17. It reminds us of the harvest that used to be brought to the Temple during Sukkot

18. Passover and Shavuot

19. The first seven

20. a) Hag (Festival of Joy)
    b) Z'man Simhateynu (Season of our Rejoicing)
    c) Hag Ha-Asif (Festival of Ingathering)

21. The words mean "many hoshanas"—all the Hoshanas of the previous days are recited then

22. a) The Water-Pouring Festival
    b) During the days of the Second Temple

23. Sh'mini Atzeret is my Hebrew name
    a) What is it in English?
    b) When am I observed?

24. Name two prayers which make Sh'mini Atzeret a serious day.

25. Why do we pray for rain on Sh'mini Atzeret?

26. I am the jolliest day of the Fall Festivals. Who am I?

27. Why are we happy on Simhat Torah?

23. a) Eighth Day of Solemn Assembly
    b) On the 8th day of the Sukkot Festival

24. The prayers for rain and the Yizkor (memorial prayer) for the departed

25. This festival marks the beginning of the rainy season in Israel

26. Simhat Torah

27 We celebrate the finishing and the beginning of the reading of the Torah

28. How many times, and when, is the Torah read on Simhat Torah?

29. a) Which portions of the Torah are read on Simhat Torah?
    b) Why is it done this way?

30. What are the Hakafot?

31. How many times are the Torah scrolls carried during the Hakafot?

32. What do the children do as they march in the processions?

33. Why is the Torah reading repeated so many times on Simhat Torah?

34. All the children are standing under a large Talit. Can you name the ceremony?

35. What is meant by *Hattan Torah* and *Hattan B'reshit*?

36. How many names for Sukkot can you give?

28. Twice. Once in the evening and once in the morning

29. a) The very last and then immediately after, the very first again
    b) To show that reading the Torah never ends

30. The processions with the Torah scrolls around the synagogue

31. Seven times

32. Carry flags and apples

33. In order to give every man in the synagogue an opportunity to be called up to the Torah

34. Kol Ha-n'arim (All the Boys)

35. *Hattan Torah*—the honor of calling up men for the reading of the very last part of the Torah
    Hattan B'reshit—the same, but for reading the very first part of the Torah

36. Z'man Simhateynu
    Hag Ha—Asif
    Hag Ha-Sukkot

HANUKKA

(*Courtesy Israel Information Services.*)

No doubt you already know something about Hanukka and have observed some of its customs. You probably know that we light candles, play games, exchange gifts, etc. But you may not know just why we do all these things and may not be familiar with the ways in which we celebrate it. We will therefore give here a brief summary in answer to the two questions: WHY do we observe Hanukka? and HOW do we observe it?

The WHY comes first and gives a brief summary of the story of Hanukka. However, since this provides the barest facts, we hope you will try to learn more about this beautiful festival by reading some of the material listed in "For Further Reading."

The HOW tells some of the different ways of observing and enjoying the Hanukka festival. This too is but a brief outline of the observances. Additional reading will supply much meaningful information.

In addition to special Hebrew terms and numbers, you will also find here short Hanukka stories, "More Hanukka Lights," and blessings and hymns for Hanukka. Don't miss any of these!

A HAPPY HANUKKA!

THE STORY OF HANUKKA—
WHY WE CELEBRATE IT

As we celebrate this colorful eight-day festival of Hanukka, we light candles each night. It is a happy festival and brings enjoyment to all. However, it is interesting to recall how it began and why it became a holiday. You will be surprised at the story these lovely little candles have to tell.

For this we must go back 2100 years to the time when our forefathers were living in their own land, Israel, but under the rule of mighty Syria. Everything went along as usual until the throne fell to a cruel king named Antiochus (also called "The Madman"). He decided to force the Jews, together with all other peoples over whom he reigned, to follow the Greek religion—and no other. The Jews were not allowed to live as the Torah teaches us; they were ordered to worship Greek gods and to behave like the Greeks in other ways as well.

The Jews, of course, would not accept this; they decided to rebel and fight the Syrians. An aged priest named Mattathias, who lived in the town of Modin (near Jerusalem), was their leader. He, together with his five sons and other brave volunteers, began fighting against the mighty Syrian armies.

When, about a year later, Mattathias died, his son Judah (called the "Maccabee") took his place as the leader. Because he was a very clever general, Judah and his small force were able to fight for three years and in the end they defeated the Syrians. Even though Judah's army was much smaller than that of the Syrians, the Jews won. Why? Because they fought with God in their hearts and with full faith in His power to save them. They were ready to give their lives for their religion so that they might worship God according to their own beliefs.

After the victory Judah and his men went into the Temple in Jerusalem and cleansed it of all the Greek gods and idols that the Syrians had placed there. When it was purified they wanted to light the large menora. But they could find no container of oil bearing the seal of the High Priest. (No other oil was permitted for this purpose.) Finally, someone did find a small jar of oil, which, however, was enough for only one day. But God performed a miracle: the small jar of oil burned for eight days, by which time more of the pure oil had been prepared. This miracle, coming on the heels of the military victory, cheered the people greatly and they celebrated with joyous thanks.

To remind ourselves of this wonderful miracle, and, to keep alive the feeling that we Jews are always ready to fight for our right to worship God as the Torah teaches us—for these two reasons we light candles on each successive Hanukka night.*

The Six-Day War in June 1967 and the Yom Kippur War of 1973 are more recent examples of the Jew's courage in the face of probable defeat. There is no doubt that the Israelis defeated their Arab enemies only because they were inspired by the same faith in God as were their Maccabean ancestors. Therefore, as we light our candles each Hanukka night, let us keep in mind all the brave Jews who fought and died so that we today might live and enjoy living as proud, free and happy Jews, setting a worthy example for other peoples to follow.

HOW DO WE OBSERVE HANUKKA?

The story of Hanukka tells us *why* we observe it. Let us now see what are some of the enjoyable ways of observing it.

The first and best known way is lighting candles on eight successive evenings. We begin with one on the first night, then add one more each night after that. Every candle is lighted with the *Shammash*, a special candle which "serves" the others. Immediately after the candles are lit, everyone joins in the singing of the two Hanukka hymns, *Maoz Tzur* and *Ha-Nerot Halalu*. The candle lighting ceremony always takes place after dark, except on Friday, when they are kindled just before those for the Sabbath (so that no fire will be handled after the Sabbath has begun).

Since Hanukka is a minor festival (not having been commanded by Moses in the Torah) work is permitted during the festival.

As on every holiday, on Hanukka some special prayers are recited. They are:

1. The *AL HA-NISIM*, in which we tell why we observe this festival, with special stress on the great miracle, and

2. The *HALLEL*, the prayer in which we praise our God with great joy for having saved our forefathers by this miraculous victory. In addition, the Torah is read every day of Hanukka, the selection being a special portion from the Book of Numbers.

The Hanukka games are especially popular. The favorite is the *dreidl* game. The dreidl (Hanukka spinning top) contains four sides; on each side is found one of the following letters: *Nun, Gimmel, Hay* and *Shin*.

---

* Additional reasons for observing Hanukka for eight days are given in "More Hanukka Lights," pp. 73-4.

These letters stand for the words found in one of our Hanukka prayers: Nays Gadol Haya Shom ("A great miracle occurred there"). If the dreidl falls on the Nun, the player gets nothing; if it falls on the Gimmel, the player takes the whole pot; if on the Hay, the player takes half; if it falls on the Shin, he must put up the amount agreed upon at the start of the game.

A favorite food is associated with every festival. Hanukka is no exception; on this holiday we eat *latkes* (pancakes).*

Then, after the meal, it is customary to play cards. Many an observant Jew who does not believe in playing cards throughout the year, will usually do so on Hanukka.

Gifts too are a part of Hanukka. On the fifth night gifts are usually presented to relatives and friends, although they may be presented on any other day of Hanukka as well. In addition the children are given *Hanukka Gelt*, money for Hanukka.

We observe this lovely Festival of Lights in all these different ways so that we may enjoy it to the full, keeping it alive as a reminder that we Jews believe in freedom of religion, not only for ourselves, but for all peoples.

---

* To find the reason for eating latkes on Hanukka, see "More Hanukka Lights," pp. 73-4.

Hanukka in a Bucharian home in Jerusalem.
(Courtesy Keren Hayesod.)

SOME HANUKKA TALES

HANNAH AND HER SEVEN SONS

During the war against the Syrians a certain Jewess named Hannah, along with her seven sons, were once arrested by the Syrian officers, who then tried to keep them from following the Jewish laws. First they were ordered to eat meat that was *unkosher* (forbidden to Jews) but every one of them refused to do so.

Next a high Syrian officer set up a Greek idol and commanded each of Hannah's son to bow to it. He began with the oldest son, who refused. Then, as each son in turn refused to bow down to the idol, he was sent off to be tortured and killed.

Finally, when the turn of the youngest son came, the officer said to him, "Look, son, I won't ask you to bow down to this idol because I don't want your mother to be left without at least one son. So let's do this: I am going to drop my ring in front of the idol, and you just pick it up and give it to me. That's all you have to do!"

But this child too refused to obey the officer, knowing that by bending down to pick up the ring, he would be bowing down to the idol. He also was sent off to die.

Hannah, now left without any children, killed herself. However, just before she jumped off a roof to her death, she cried aloud to God:

"Oh, Lord, our father Abraham was ready to, but in the end didn't have to sacrifice his son, his only son, to You. But I have given You all seven of my sons! If it had to be done, at least they died for the sake of Your great and Holy name! Blessed art Thou, the One and Only God, Who lives forever!"

It was acts of sacrifice of this kind that inspired the Jews to fight for and defend their religion—their most prized possession.

ELEAZAR

A famous Hebrew Scribe named Eleazar, was also ordered to eat forbidden meat. However, because Eleazar was an old man whom the Syrian officers in charge had known for a long time, they said to him:

"Instead of eating the non-kosher meat, you may eat kosher meat. But we will tell everyone that you are eating non-kosher meat. In that way you won't have to die." To this Eleazar replied:

"No, I won't do that! Because, if I do, I will be deceiving my people and setting the wrong example for them. Then, all the Jews may do the same and become sinners. No, I would rather die than make sinners of my fellow Jews!"

He was then immediately put to death. But the noble example that he set by remaining loyal to Judaism at all costs, spurred the Jews to fight against the Syrians more bravely than ever.

THE THOUSAND IN A CAVE

During the war against the Syrians many of the people hid in the numerous caves that abound in the mountains of Judea. Once when the king's officers found out that large groups of Jews, about a thousand of them, were hiding in a certain huge cave, they sent soldiers up there to attack them. It was the Sabbath day. The officers called to the people in the cave: "Come out and bow down to the idols, as the King commanded you. In that way you will be allowed to live. Otherwise you will die!"

The people shouted from the cave: "No, we won't come out! And we won't take up arms and break the Sabbath. We would rather die instead!" The Syrian soldiers then attacked and killed every one of the thousand Jews.

After this tragedy, Mattathias the Priest instructed his people that from then on, should they be attacked on the Sabbath day, they were permitted to defend themselves. (Jewish law allows the breaking of the Sabbath only if one's life is in real danger, because Judaism holds human life to be very precious and worth saving.)

MORE HANUKKA LIGHTS

(Less known facts about Hanukka)

In addition to the familiar tales that the eight candles of Hanukka can tell us, there are many more points about this glorious festival that are less known, yet important for a clearer understanding of Hanukka. A few such facts follow. Test yourself—how many did you know before? They will make your Hanukka lights shine more brightly for you.

1. *Why eight days of Hanukka and one candle for each night?*
   A) After the war, while some Jewish soldiers were entering the Temple, they found eight unused spears lying outside. They set them up, poured oil over them, and lighted them, thus making of them eight candles. In this way these eight spears served as a temporary *menora* while the Temple was being cleansed for worship.
   B) Since the Festival of Sukkot (an eight day major festival) could not be observed that year while the war was in progress, Hanukka was meant to serve as a sort of "second Sukkot." During the rededication ceremonies of the Temple, the Jews marched around with palm branches in their hands—just as we do on Sukkot.
   C) The students of Hillel and Shammai (two outstanding scholars) disagreed on the order of the lighting of the Hanukka candles. The students of Hillel thought we should light one candle on the first night, two on the second night, and so on through the eighth night. But Shammai's students thought the opposite; they favored lighting eight on the first night, seven on the second night, and so on to the one candle on the eighth night. In the end the decision of the school of Hillel won out, so that it is their practice that is followed: starting with one candle, we increase the number daily on to the eighth evening.

2. *Why does Hanukka begin on the 25th of Kislev?*
   Because Judah Maccabee wanted the Temple to be rededicated on the exact day it had become unclean three years earlier.

3. *Why no fasting?*
   All fasting is forbidden on Hanukka.

4. *Why did Judah succeed Mattathias?*
   Just before Mattathias died he appointed his son, Judah (the Maccabee) to be commander of the army.

5. *Are all the candles the same?*
   Except for the Shammash, all eight candles must be placed in a straight row so that none of them will seem superior to any of the others.

6. *Don't blow them out!*
   We are not allowed to blow out any of the eight candles before they burn out except for the Shammash. It may be re-used if necessary, although it is much more desirable to use a new Shammash every night.

7. *More for outsiders than for yourself.*
   The lighted Hanukka candles are meant to serve as a reminder of the miracles, wars, etc. and are therefore to be placed in a window or other spot where they may be seen by people outside our homes, so that they too will be reminded of the tales they tell.

8. *Why a Shammash?*
   Since we are not allowed to make any use of the Hanukka candles after they are lit (as for reading, lighting a darkened room, etc.), only the Shammash may be used for such a purpose. The eight candles are only to be looked at and not to be put to a practical use.

9. *Why latkes on Hanukka?*
   It is said that once during the war, while Judah and his men were pursuing the Syrians, they came to a small town feeling tired and hungry. They needed food and rest very badly but they could not stay there long enough for a full meal because they did not want the Syrians to get too far away from them. Someone then suggested that they make pancakes, or "latkes", which would be ready quickly and at the same time be filling and nourishing. Since then latkes have become the favorite food for Hanukka.

HANUKKA TERMS

AL HA-NISIM	A special prayer for Hanukka
ANTIOCHUS	The Syrian king who forbade the Jews to practice their religion
CHAG HA-UREEM	"Festival of Lights," another name for Hanukka
DREIDL	A four-sided top used in Hanukka games
ELEAZAR	A famous scribe who died as a martyr for his religion at the hands of the Syrians
EMMAUS	The place where the Jews gained a major victory over the Syrians
HALLEL	A festival prayer recited on Hanukka
HA-NEROT HALALU	One of the hymns sung after the candle-lighting on Hanukka
HANNAH	A brave Jewess whose seven sons died for their religion
HANUKKA	"Dedication," the most familiar name for this festival
HANUKKA GELT	Money given to children as a gift on Hanukka
HANUKKIAH	The Hebrew for a Hanukka menora
HELLENISTS	Those Jews who sided with the Syrian-Greeks and adopted Greek ways and customs
HIGH PRIEST	The priest in charge of the service in the Temple in Jerusalem
JERUSALEM	The city where the Temple stood
JUDAH (JUDAS)	The son of Mattathias. As general of the Jewish armies, he led the Jews to final victory over the Syrians
KISLEV	The Hebrew month in which Hanukka begins
LATKES	Pancakes, the favorite Hanukka food
MACCABEE	The name given to Judah and later to his family and descendants. (See also "MEE CHAMOCHAH")
MAOZ TZUR	One of the popular hymns sung after the lighting of Hanukka candles

MATTATHIAS	The old priest, father of Judah, who first started the war against the Syrians
MEECHAMOCHAH BA'ELIM ADONAY	"Who is like unto Thee, O Lord?"—the battle-cry of Judah and his men. Also the initial letters (in Hebrew) form the word "MACCABEE"
MODIN	The home of Mattathias and his family and the town where the war against the Syrians began
NUMBERS, BOOK OF	The fourth of the Five Books of Moses, which contains the daily Torah readings for Hanukka
NUN, GIMMEL, HAY & SHIN	The Hebrew letters on the dreidl
SHAMMASH	The special candle which lights all the others
TEVET	The Hebrew month in which Hanukka ends

Carrying a Hanukka torch.
(Courtesy Israel Information Services.)

HANUKKA NUMBERS

Less than nothing   What you get if the deidl falls on SHIN
                                        (you must put up the amount agreed upon)

Nothing   What you get if the dreidl falls on NUN

½—*Half* the pot   What you get if the dreidl falls on HAY

- 1   Only *one* Shammash
  On the *first* night we say 3 blessings
  The Shehecheyanu blessing is said only on the *first* night

- 2   Only *two* blessings are recited each night after the first
  Last day of Hanukka can fall on the *2nd* of Tevet

- 3   *Three* blessings are said on the first night
  The war lasted *three* years
  Some years, the last day of Hanukka falls on the *3rd* of Tevet

- 4   *Four* sides to the dreidl

- 5   Mattathias had *five* sons

- 7   Hannah's *seven* sons

- 8   The *eight* days of Hanukka, which are represented by *8* candles
  The menorah has *eight* branches

- 9   There is a total of *nine* candles including the Shammash
  Kislev is the *9th* month of the year

- 10   The *tenth* month of the year is Tevet (when Hanukka ends)

- 25   Hanukka begins on the *25th* day of Kislev

- 44   There are *44* candles in a box for Hanukka

- 165   The Temple was rededicated in the year *165* B.C.E.

- 2,100   Hanukka took place *2100* years ago

- 100%   Your total winnings, if the dreidl falls on GIMMEL

QUIZ QUESTIONS FOR HANUKKA

QUESTIONS: *ANSWERS:*

1. During which Hebrew month does Hanukka begin?
2. What is the full Hebrew date of Hanukka?
3. What does the term "Hanukka" mean?
4. How many blessings do we say on the first night of Hanukka?
5. What are they?
6. How many blessings are recited on the 2nd and the following nights of Hanukka?
7. What are they?
8. For how many days does Hanukka last?
9. Name the candle which lights all the others.
10. About how long ago did the story of Hanukka take place?
11. Who was Mattathias?
12. How many sons did Mattathias have?
13. How did Judah become famous?
14. Why was Judah called Maccabee?

1. Kislev
2. 25th of Kislev to the 2nd or 3rd of Tevet
3. a) Dedication
   b) Chanu (they rested) kah (on the 25th)
4. Three
5. a) L'hadlik nayr shel Hanukka
   b) She-asa-nisim
   c) She-he-che-yanu
6. Two
7. The first two (see answer #5)
8. For eight days
9. The Shammash candle
10. About 2100 years ago, in the year 165 B.C.E.
11. Father of Judah, the one who started the war against the Syrians
12. Five sons
13. He led the Jews to victory over the Syrians
14. a) Maccabee means "hammer"
    b) Also because it forms the initials of the Hebrew words: "Mee Chamochah Ba-elim Adonay"

15. Why did it seem foolish for the Jews to fight against the Syrians?

15. Because the Syrians had a much larger and stronger army than the Jews had

16. Why did the Jews decide to fight against the Syrians?

16. Because the Syrian King forbade them to teach and to practice their religion

17. What did Judah and his men find in the Temple when they first returned there after the war?

17. Greek idols and sacrifices

18. Why couldn't ordinary oil be used in the Temple?

18. It had to have the seal of the High Priest on it

19. Name the books where much of the story of Hanukka is found.

19. The two Books of the Maccabees

20. What was Modin?

20. The town where the war began

21. Who was Antiochus?

21. The Syrian king who wouldn't allow the Jews to follow their religion

22. Why is Hanukka a minor festival?

22. Because it was not commanded by Moses in the Torah

23. Why do we observe Hanukka for eight days?

23. a) The oil found in the Temple lasted for eight days
b) The eight spears, covered with oil, that were lit and became a temporary menora
c) Hanukka served as a sort of "Second Sukkot," the eight-day festival which couldn't be celebrated that year while the war was still on and the Syrians held the Temple

24. Name the four letters on the dreidl.

24. NUN, GIMMEL, HAY, SHIN— the initials for the words: NAYS GADOL HAYA SHOM (A great miracle occurred there)

25. What is meant by "Hanukka Gelt"?

25. Money given on Hanukka

26. Name the favorite Hanukka food.

26. Latkes, or pancakes

27. What is the value of each letter on the dreidl when playing the game?

27. *NUN*—nothing; *GIMMEL*—all; *HAY*—half of the pot; *SHIN*—put up

28. On which night of Hanukka are gifts usually presented?

28. On the fifth night

29. What is Al Ha-Nisim?

29. A special prayer said on Hanukka

30. Which popular game is often played during Hanukka?

30. Cards

31. Name a special prayer which is also recited on Hanukka.

31. The Hallel prayer

32. For what basic rights did the Jews fight the Syrians?

32. Freedom of religion

33. a) When, on Hanukka, are the candles to be lit?
    b) When are they not to be lit after dark?
    c) In which direction are they to be lit?

33. a) Every night after dark
    b) On Friday night, and then, just before lighting the Shabbat candles
    c) From left to right, lighting the new candle first each night

34. How many candles are there in a box?

34. 44

35. What are the Maoz Tzur and Hanerot Halalu?

35. Hymns sung after lighting the candles

36. What was Emmaus?

36. The place where a famous battle with the Syrians took place

37. a) Who was Hannah?
    b) Why were her sons put to death?

37. a) A brave Jewess whose seven sons died for their religion
    b) Because they refused to bow down before the Greek idols or to eat forbidden food

38. The Maccabean victory in 165 B.C.E. gave complete political independence to the Jews. What is wrong with this statement?

38. The Maccabean victory of 165 B.C.E. meant only religious freedom for the Jews. Complete political independence didn't come until about 20 years later.

39. Mordecai is a Purim hero. How is he connected with Hanukka?

39. In the song, "Maoz Tzur," the initial letters of the first five verses form the word MORDECAI (probably the name of the author of the song)

TU BISHVAT

*Planting the trees in Israel on Tu Bishvat.
(Courtesy Israel Information Services.)*

    Among the least-known of all our holidays is Tu Bishvat (Jewish Arbor Day). As you will soon see it is not a religious holiday, yet it is a very ancient one and connected with trees. Why has it lasted and survived for so long if we aren't required to observe it? The answer is in the WHY portion of this chapter along with something of the history and background of Tu Bishvat. The HOW section tells of the various ways it was celebrated, both in ancient and in modern times.

    Included here are only the significant facts. There is much more to be learned about Tu Bishvat. Read additional information as well as some stories in the books listed under "For Further Reading."

ENJOY YOUR TU BISHVAT!

WHY WE OBSERVE TU BISHVAT

One of the oldest holidays that we observe without being commanded to do so, is Tu Bishvat, which deals mostly with trees and with the land of Israel. Even though it began in Bible times and even though for thousands of years since then most Jews didn't even live in Israel, they still continued to observe it regularly. Why is this so? Because the Jew always had a strong love for Israel no matter where he lived.

You will be better able to understand the Tu Bishvat holiday if you examine its different names. *Tu Bishvat* is the Hebrew for the 15th day of the Hebrew month of Shvat (which usually falls in January or February). The word *Tu* means fifteen because it is composed of the two letters *tet*, which equals 9, and *vav*, which equals 6. In Bible times this was the last day for paying the tithe or ten-percent tax due to the Temple in Jerusalem. This tax had to be paid on all crops produced on the farm. After the 15th of Shvat any fruit on which the tithe had not been paid was not allowed to be eaten. Another name for the festival is *Hamishah Asar Bishvat* which also means the fifteenth of Shvat written out in Hebrew words

According to a certain Jewish belief the trees are judged by God on this day just as all men are judged on Rosh HaShana. From this comes its third name, *Rosh HaShana L'Ilanot* (New Year for the Trees). Just as God decides the fate of every human on Rosh HaShana, so does He determine whether a tree will bloom and grow, wither or be cut down, be well-watered or dry, etc.

However, Tu Bishvat is also the time when Spring begins in Israel and the trees take on new life and growth. It has, therefore, become a specific day for tree-planting there, giving special expression to the Jew's natural love of trees. In fact, the Torah itself is known as a "Tree of Life" which always continues to "give forth its fruit in its season." It used to be considered as great a crime to chop down a live tree as to kill a human being. Here are a few Bible quotations which show us how deep the Jew's love for trees has always been.

"When you come into the Land, you shall plant all kinds of trees for food." (Leviticus, 19:23)

"When you shall besiege a city, you shall not cut its trees with an ax ...... you may eat of them, but you shall not cut them down." (Deuteronomy, 20:19)

"It (The Torah) is a Tree of Life to those who take hold of it." (Proverbs, 3:18)

"The fruit of a righteous (man) is a Tree of Life." (Proverbs, 11:30)

The Jew grew to love not only trees, but also the land where he planted many trees. This was his homeland, Israel. Therefore, when we observe Tu Bishvat we show our love for Israel and our desire to make it the one and only real home for the Jew. That is why we Jews have observed this beautiful festival through the ages, even though during the dark days of the Middle Ages, and other painful eras, many a Jew never saw a tree or expected to go to Israel. In our own day the State of Israel has more meaning for us, especially because now it is again our homeland, the true home of the Jews. Today we feel closer to Israel than ever before, particularly since travel to that land is easier and more common now than it has ever been. Finally, the Six-Day War (during June 5-10, 1967) gave the State of Israel higher prestige and standing among the nations of the world than it had at any other time in history.

Therefore, always remember, that as trees are being planted in Israel, they are being planted not only for the Israelis, but also for you, for all of us Jews wherever we may be. This in turn should also remind you that the land with all those beautiful trees must always grow and prosper. Let it always bloom and be fruitful so that it will continue to be a land to which every Jew everywhere can turn with pride. This is the message of Tu Bishvat. Let us heed it and share our joy of that day with our fellow-Jews in Israel and throughout the world.

HOW TU BISHVAT IS OBSERVED

Since this lovely little holiday centers chiefly around Israel, it is but natural that tree-planting should be the most important manner of observing it. Ever since we were commanded in the Bible, "And when you shall come into the land and shall have planted every kind of tree for food" (Leviticus, 19:23), our people have always planted many trees in Israel. But later Tu Bishvat was chosen as the special day for tree-planting.

In fact, in Israel, in ancient times, there existed a custom of planting a tree on Tu Bishvat whenever a child was born. A cedar tree was planted for a boy, and for a girl—a cypress tree. Then when the children grew up and married, the branches from each of their trees were used for the *huppah* or bridal canopy. In this way both birth and marriages were connected with trees, and the Jew grew up with a love for them.

Today, in modern Israel, Tu Bishvat is an official holiday (though not a religious one) and, of course, also a school holiday. The children take the leading part in most of the ceremonies, especially in the tree-planting. These ceremonies feature elaborate parades, songs, dances and general merriment. During the tree-planting ceremonies, each child plants his own sapling. (For a more detailed description of the tree-planting ceremony in Tel-Aviv, read Ben H. Edidin's *Jewish Holidays and Festivals*, pages 111-114.)

In lands outside of Israel, Tu Bishvat is observed in a different way. For one thing, it is customary to eat Israeli fruit, which is one way of reminding us not only of this festival, but also of our love for Israel. Then, also, parties and other celebrations are held in schools, synagogues, Jewish centers, etc. In the schools special assemblies and parties are held, often followed by planting one or more trees.

Having a tree planted in Israel is another way of observing Tu Bishvat. Thus, by buying a Jewish National Fund tree certificate, you can have a tree planted there either in honor or in memory of anyone you wish. This custom also brings us closer to Israel and reminds us of what it means to us. The trees thus planted naturally help to build up the land.

But all of these, and other, customs all serve to forge another link between us and the land of Israel. Tu Bishvat thus reminds us to continue to study more about our homeland and to do our bit in supporting it and always keeping it alive in our hearts.

When we look back over the history of the rise and growth of modern Israel during the last fifty or sixty years, we often wonder how this all-but-impossible task was accomplished in such a short period of time. The many stories of the devotion and heroism of the Halutzim (pioneers) may seem to be unbelievable, but all of these great achievements (including the increase in population from a mere handful to more than 2,500,000 at present) were made possible only because of the Jew's undying hope and stubborn determination to reclaim his homeland as his own.

On Tu Bishvat, Israel's tree-planting day, let us remember that the land we are honoring is our land; its people are our people; its language, Hebrew, is our language; and its history is one which all of us Jews share in common. Ties such as these keep Israel alive for us, not merely one day a year, but every day and every moment of our lives.

HAVE AN ENJOYABLE TU BISHVAT!

An ancient oak tree in Israel.
(Courtesy Jewish National Fund.)

TERMS FOR TU BISHVAT
(AND FOR ISRAEL IN GENERAL)

ALIYAH	immigration to Israel
ALMOND TREE	the first tree to bloom in Israel
CEDAR TREE	planted in honor of a baby boy
CHAIM WEIZMANN	first president of the State of Israel
CHONI HA-MA'AGEL	the man who slept for 70 years
CYPRESS TREE	planted in honor of a baby girl
EMEK	Hebrew for "Valley," usually refers to the Emek Yizrael, a famous valley of many agricultural settlements
EUCALYPTUS TREE	a tree imported into Israel from Mexico; its roots drain swamps
HAIFA	Israel's third largest city, famous as a port
HALUTZ	a pioneer in Israel
HAMISHAH ASAR BISHVAT	same as Tu Bishvat
HUPPAH	a marriage canopy, under which a bride and groom stand for their wedding ceremony
ISRAEL BONDS	certificates received for lending money to Israel
JERUSALEM	capital of Israel
JEWISH NATIONAL FUND	an organization that raises money for the development and growth of the Land of Israel
KEREN KAYEMET L'YISROEL	Hebrew name for the Jewish National Fund
KNESSET	Israel's law-making body
NAHALAH	legal right to land bought in Israel
ROSH HASHANA L'ILANOT	"New Year for the Trees" (another name for this festival)
TEL AVIV	largest city in Israel
THEODOR HERZL	first president of the Zionist Movement
TITHE	the 10% tax due for all farm produce during the days of the Temple

"TREE OF LIFE"	a term describing the Torah
TU BISHVAT	15th of month of Shvat (a name of this festival)
ZIONISM	a movement which seeks to bring Jews back to Israel and to settle them there

TU BISHVAT NUMBERS

Tell how each of the following numbers refers to Tu Bishvat or to Israel.

1	*First* President of Israel—Chaim Weizmann
	First nation to recognize the State of Israel—United States
	First Aliyah—in 1882
	First tree to bloom in Israel—the almond tree
3	Israel's *3* largest cities: Tel Aviv, Jerusalem, Haifa
6	The *Vav* of Tu Bishvat
9	The *Tet* of Tu Bishvat
11	Shvat is the *11th* month of the year
15	*15th* of Shvat
20 plus	Years since Israel became an Independent State in 1948
70	Years that Choni slept
2,000,000 plus—Jews in Israel
10's of millions—Trees planted in Israel

SOME OF THE TREES AND SHRUBS THAT GROW IN ISRAEL

1. Acacia
2. Almond
3. Apple
4. Apricot
5. Banana
6. Carob
7. Cedar
8. Cypress
9. Eucalyptus
10. Fig
11. Lime
12. Myrtle
13. Oak
14. Olive
15. Orange
16. Palm
17. Peach
18. Pepper
19. Pine
20. Vine
21. Walnut

QUIZ QUESTIONS FOR TU BISHVAT

QUESTIONS:

1. What is the meaning of the words "Tu Bishvat"?
2. Where is Tu Bishvat celebrated as a full holiday?
3. Give the Hebrew names for Jewish Arbor Day.
4. How do Jews living outside of Israel observe Tu Bishvat?

5. What meaning do the Hebrew letters *Tet, Vav* in Tu Bishvat have?
6. How does Tu Bishvat differ from such festivals as Rosh HaShana or Sukkot?
7. When a boy was born in ancient times, what kind of tree was planted in his honor?
8. What is the meaning of the words "Rosh HaShana L'Ilanot"?
9. With what kind of tree was the birth of a girl celebrated?
10. What was done with the trees planted for a boy and a girl when they grew up and married?
11. How can a Jew outside Israel have a tree planted in the land of Israel?
12. Who takes the important part in the tree-planting ceremony in Israel on Tu Bishvat?
13. Give the Hebrew meaning for Jewish National Fund.

ANSWERS:

1. The 15th of the Hebrew month of Shvat
2. In Israel
3. Tu Bishvat, Hamishah Asar Bishvat, Rosh Hashana L'Ilanot
4. a) By eating Israeli fruits on that day
   b) By having trees planted in Israel and by celebrations
5. They stand for the number 15; *Tet* for nine, *Vav* for six
6. Tu Bishvat is not a religious holiday

7. A cedar tree

8. New Year of the Trees

9. A cypress tree

10. Its branches were used for making their bridal canopy (huppah)

11. By buying a tree certificate

12. The school children

13. Keren Kayemet L'Yisroel

14. What is the work of the Jewish National Fund?

14. To buy and develop the land in Israel for the people of Israel, such as opening up areas for settlements, planting millions of trees, building roads, etc.

15. Name some types of trees grown in Israel.

15. Almond, Cedar, Fig, Date, Carob, Vine

16. Who is commonly known as the Jewish "Rip Van Winkle"?

16. Choni Ha-Ma'agel

17. Why is the Emek so famous?

17. It was turned into a most fertile spot after having been swampland for many years

18. What is a nahalah?

18. A title to land bought in Israel

19. Which is the first tree to blossom in Israel?

19. The almond tree

20. How long did Choni sleep?

20. For seventy years

21. In which Jewish writings are the Israelites commanded to plant trees?

21. In the Bible

22. Name the largest river in Israel.

22. The River Jordan

23. For what reason was Tu Bishvat so important during ancient times?

23. It was the last day on which to pay the tithe (a 10% tax) due to the Levites

24. What are four reasons that trees are now planted in Israel?

24. For fruit, shade, buildings and draining of swamps

25. Name the tree that was imported into Israel in order to drain the swamps.

25. The Eucalyptus tree, from Mexico

26. Who was Dr. Theodor Herzl?

26. Founder of the Zionist Movement

27. What is the exact birthday of the present State of Israel?

27. May 14, 1948 (5th of Iyar, 5708)

28. Name the first President of the State of Israel.

28. Chaim Weizmann

29. What do all the following terms have in common: Blue Box, Golden Book, Tree Fund, Flag Day?

29. All of them are ways of raising money for the Jewish National Fund

30. Which nation was the first to officially recognize the State of Israel?	30. The United States
31. When did the first Aliyah (mass immigration) to Israel begin?	31. In 1882
32. How many Jews now live in the State of Israel?	32. About two and a half million
33. Name the law-making body of Israel that corresponds to the Congress of the United States.	33. The Knesset
34. What is the capital city of Israel?	34. Jerusalem
35. Name the largest city in Israel.	35. Tel Aviv
36. What are Israel Bonds?	36. Bonds bought to support the State of Israel, repaid after a number of years by Israel's government
37. Where does spring begin first in Israel, in the highlands or the lowlands?	37. In the lowlands

An old olive tree.

PURIM

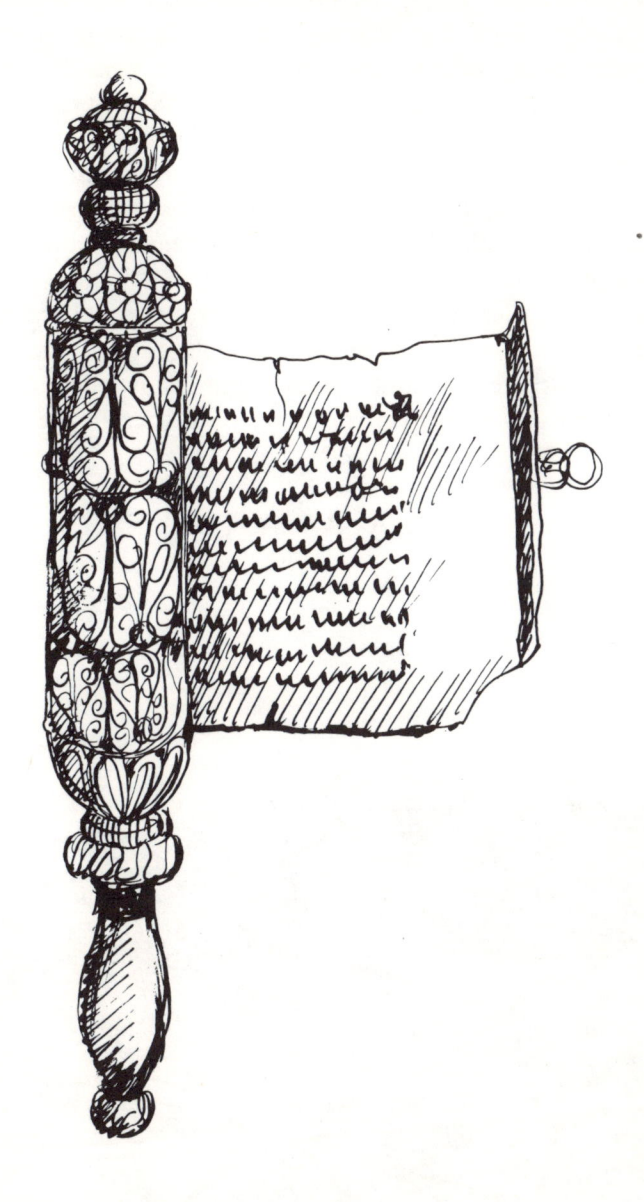

When Purim was declared a holiday, it was meant to be a day of merriment and remembering. For these and other reasons it has been observed continuously for thousands of years. But, you may ask, what is so joyous about Purim and what is there to be remembered?

To answer these and other questions, the WHY portion tells the dramatic tale of Purim. Then, the HOW section brings a number of ways in which this gay festival has delighted our people for so many generations.

These sections provide a very general idea of what Purim is all about, while the additional material, Purim "Terms," "Numbers" and "Legends," offers more information to be used in a variety of ways.

After absorbing all of these, you should be ready to join your fellow-Jews in really enjoying Purim, one of the jolliest of festivals. Experiences such as these help to make Judaism a most exciting adventure in living. The fun you have on Purim will never be forgotten.

But of course, there are many other interesting and exciting things to know about Purim. Reading some of the books listed under "For Further Reading" will help deepen and clarify your knowledge of this holiday. The complete story is related in the Book of Esther in the Bible. It might be best to read that first.

HAVE A JOLLY PURIM!

A Purim grogger.

WHY WE OBSERVE PURIM

A miracle is connected with two of our happy holidays—Hanukka and Purim. But it is Purim that is our gayest festival. It is based on one of the most interesting tales told by our people. Here it is, in brief.

Over 2,000 years ago, there ruled in Persia a mighty king named Ahasuerus. One time this king (whose empire consisted of 127 provinces), having been angered by his queen, Vashti, sent her away, and began to search for a new queen. To this end he let it be known throughout his kingdom that all beautiful maidens were to be brought to his palace in Shushan, the capital. There he would choose one of them to be his new queen.

Now, in this capital city of Shushan, lived a learned Jew named Mordecai. He had a young cousin, Esther, whom he had raised as his own daughter after the death of her parents. Mordecai advised Esther, who was very beautiful, to join the other maidens in the hope that she might be chosen queen. And sure enough, she became the new queen. From then on Mordecai often visited the palace grounds to see her and speak with her.

But shortly after this, King Ahasuerus appointed as his prime minister a man named Haman. This man, who was very vain and proud, commanded that everyone seeing him must bow down to him. Mordecai, being an observant Jew, naturally refused to do this. His refusal made Haman very angry and, as a result, he persuaded the King to sign a law ordering all the Jews of his vast empire to be put to death on a certain day that would be chosen by Haman. After casting lots, Haman chose the 13th day of the month of Adar.

The Jews, of course, were very frightened by this decree, and Mordecai immediately begged Esther to go to the King to help save her people. At first she hesitated since no one (not even she, the queen) was allowed to come before the King without having been asked. But, after Mordecai had warned her that if this decree was to be carried out, she too would be killed, she agreed to obey Mordecai to risk her life for the sake of her people. But first, she told Mordecai, all the Jews must fast and pray, just as she and her maidens were going to do for three days.

In the meantime, Esther had informed Ahasuerus of a plot (which had been overheard by Mordecai) that two of his guards had made against the

King's life. As a reward for having reported this plot, Mordecai was royally honored by being paraded through the streets of Shushan seated on a horse led by Haman, the Prime Minister.

Finally, Esther came before the King one night when, fortunately, he was in a good mood and received her very affectionately. He then asked her what she wanted most, promising that it would be given to her. But Esther only requested that on the following evening the King and Haman come to her rooms for a royal banquet. During the banquet, when Ahasuerus again offered to grant her every wish, she again invited the King and Haman to another feast the next evening.

But, on the third evening, when the King again repeated his previous question, she told him of Haman's plan to kill all the Jews, and also revealed that she herself was Jewish. Since Ahasuerus now loved Esther very much he immediately ordered Haman to be hanged. It so happened that the gallows on which Haman met his end was the same one which he had originally built to hang Mordecai.

However, the Jews were not yet safe. The King now had to give them weapons with which to defend themselves, since, according to the Persian law, any decree signed and sealed by the King could never be changed. The Persians therefore attacked on the day Haman had chosen by lots, but after the Jews were given weapons they defended themselves very bravely and successfully against their attackers, and won.

Mordecai was then appointed Prime Minister in place of Haman, and he proclaimed this day on which the Jews were saved as a holiday to be observed every year in remembrance of this happy and welcome miracle which saved the Jews of Persia. Esther and Mordecai then wrote all of these events in a Megilla (scroll) so that it might be read every year on the 14th day of the month of Adar, the official date of Purim.

This practice has been followed faithfully ever since and has become one of our principal ways of observing Purim. How we observe this custom, along with many others, will be told in the next section.

Even though Purim is considered a minor festival, because it was not commanded in the Torah, it is nevertheless an important minor festival since it is commanded in the Book of Esther, one of the Five Scrolls in the Holy Writings (the third section of the Bible).

HOW PURIM IS OBSERVED

Purim is invariably associated with the reading of the Megilla. A Megilla is a scroll of parchment, smaller than a Torah scroll, but written in exactly the same way. This Megilla of Esther is but one of five scrolls included in the Bible, each of which is to be read on a certain specific holiday. The Megilla of Esther is the best-known of the five.

On Purim, the Megilla must be read twice, once in the evening and again on the following morning. Every Jew is required to hear the reading both times, and every single word must be heard.

During the Megilla reading, it is customary for the children to "stamp out" the name of Haman by making a loud noise every time his name is read. The reason for this practice is that Haman was descended from the Amalekites. These people attacked the Jews just as they left Egypt, weak and defenseless. With cowardly cruelty the Amalekites even attacked women and children. God therefore commanded the Israelites to wipe out the name of Amalek. A "grogger," or "noisemaker," is generally used for making all the noise.

In addition to the Megilla reading, the synagogue services also include the "Al Ha–Nisim" prayer (similar to the one for Hanukka) thanking God for the miracle of Purim. A few other special prayers are also added, and the Torah is read.

Another precept for Purim is *Mishloach Manot* (sending of gifts) and *Matanot L'Evyonim* (gifts to the poor). For Mishloach Manot every Jew is required to send gifts of food to at least two other persons. The gifts to the poor are usually donated through some Jewish charity organization.

The favorite Purim goody is the *hammentash*, the three-cornered cake (shaped like Haman's hat) that is usually filled with poppyseed, raisins, prunes, etc. This delicacy is generally eaten during the *Seudah* (feast) which reminds us of Esther's royal banquet. This feast, which is held during the late afternoon or early evening of Purim day, is customarily a very elaborate meal, with relatives and friends also present.

Because the story of Purim is such an exciting tale, it is also most suitable for dramatization. It therefore became customary for groups of actors known as *Purim spielers* (Purim players) to go from place to place on Purim acting out the events of the Purim story.

The day before Purim is known as *Ta'anit Esther* (the Fast of Esther), a reminder of Esther's fast before she went to the King. If Purim falls on a Sunday, Ta'anit Esther is observed on the Thursday before, since fasting on Friday and on the Sabbath (except for Yom Kippur) is forbidden.

The day following Purim is called *Shushan Purim*, recalling the fact that the Jews of the city of Shushan had to fight an extra day and could therefore not celebrate Purim until one day later.

In addition to the traditional Purim festivities there are also Purim celebrations by other Jewish communities which were saved from other "Hamans" at different times. A few of these additional "Purims" are described by B. Edidin in his book *Jewish Holidays and Festivals*, page 121.

As Purim is such a jolly day, it lends itself well to parties and festivities of all kinds, especially masquerades in which characters of the Purim story are always well represented.

Joy and merriment are a most important part of celebrating Purim, and everyone must be happy on this day, since sadness on Purim is forbidden. In fact, our rabbis have said that even should we ever do away with all our other festivals, Purim is one of the few that will always remain. ". . . . and these days of Purim will never pass away from among the Jews" we are told toward the end of the Book of Esther. If we will always be merry on Purim and thereby observe it as we are commanded to, it never will.

But accompanying the fun and gaiety is our constant duty to remember Purim's message—to maintain our faith in God instead of fearing any acts of man. We thank Him for His miracle, but we never rely upon miracles. Instead, we try to show God that we are worthy of a miracle (if and when it should ever be needed) by following in His ways, dealing kindly and justly with our fellow-men, and keeping Judaism strongly alive. By following this path in life, we will make another Megilla verse come true for us: "For the Jews there was light and gladness, joy and honor." It is up to us to prove ourselves worthy of such a divine blessing.

*Purim plate, Germany, 19th century.
(Courtesy The Israel Museum, Jerusalem.)*

BRIEF BITS FROM PURIM LEGENDLAND

The following are only a very few of the many legends connected with Purim. (See H. Goldin, *The Book of Legends*, Vol. II, for more legends.)

1. Haman hated the Jews because a Jewess (Esther) had taken the place of Vashti, who was his sister.

2. He also hated Mordecai because he had at one time been Mordecai's barber, and slave.

3. Esther's father had died before her birth and her mother at her birth.

4. The name "Esther" was another name for "Venus."

5. Esther was supposed to have been forty years old when she married Ahasuerus. Some say she could have been seventy-four (from the Hebrew letters "Hadassah").

6. Mordecai had kept Esther hidden for four years before he had allowed her to go to the King's palace.

7. While Esther was in the King's palace she observed all laws of the Torah. Instead of eating meat she ate only vegetarian foods.

8. King Ahasuerus was said to have been so wealthy that he set up couches of gold and silver in the main streets of his capital so that everyone might see how rich he was.

9. It was Zeresh, Haman's wife, who advised him to hang Mordecai on a gallows, because any other way of killing him wouldn't work.

10. All the trees of the forest had refused to give their wood for Haman's gallows on which to hang Mordecai, until only the thornbush agreed and offered its wood.

11. Haman had planned to kill 22,000 school children before killing Mordecai.

12. During the night when the chronicles were read to him, two angels threw the King out of his bed 365 times in order to keep him awake.

13. One reason for Vashti's refusal to appear before the people during the seven-day feast was that she had had leprosy (a contagious skin disease) all over her body.

14. Mordecai refused to bow down to Haman because a picture of an idol had been sewn on his garment.

The following is not a legend, but is found in the Book of Esther:
After Haman was hanged, many Persians and others in the Persian Empire suddenly became Jews because of their fear that they might be killed.

TERMS FOR PURIM

ADAR	The Hebrew month during which Purim occurs
AD-LO-YA-DAH	The Purim carnival in Israel
AHASUERUS	The king of the Purim story
AL HA-NISIM	A special prayer recited on both Hanukka and Purim
AMALEKITES	The ancient people from whom Haman was descended
BENJAMIN	The tribe from which Mordecai was descended
ESTHER	King Ahasuerus' Jewish Queen, and the heroine of the Purim story
FEAST OF LOTS	Another name for Purim
THE FIVE SCROLLS	The series of shorter books of the Bible, which are read on certain festivals and fasts, and of which the Book of Esther is the most famous
GROGGER	A noisemaker used during the Megilla reading
HADASSAH	The Hebrew name of Esther
HAMAN	King Ahasuerus' prime minister who wanted all Jews to be killed in one day
HAMMENTASH	A three-cornered cake which is the favorite food for Purim
HOLY WRITINGS	The third section of the Bible which includes the Book of Esther
MATANOT L'EVYONIM	Gifts to the poor on Purim
MEGILLA	A small scroll, referring especially to the Book of Esther
MISHLOACH MANOT	The sending of gifts to one another on Purim
MORDECAI	The cousin of Esther, and the hero of the Purim story
PERSIA	The land where the Purim story took place. Today it is called Iran
PUR	A lot or a "Chance"
PURIM	The name of this festival

PURIM SPIELER	Purim actor
SEUDAH	The special Purim feast
SHALACH MONOS TRAGGER	A special bearer of Purim gifts
SHUSHAN	The capital city of Persia where the story of Purim took place
SHUSHAN PURIM	The name by which the day after Purim is known
TA'ANIT ESTHER	The Fast of Esther
VASHTI	King Ahasuerus' first queen
ZERESH	The wife of Haman

NUMBERS TO REMEMBER FOR PURIM

1	Purim lasts but *one* day
2	Mishloach Manot must be sent to at least *2* people Mordecai overheard the plot of *2* guards
3	Esther fasted for *3* days The Hammentash has *3* sides
5	The *Five* Megillot of which the Book of Esther is one
10	Haman had *10* sons
12	Purim falls during Adar, which is the *12th* month of the year
13	Haman first chose the *13th* day of Adar
14	Purim comes on the *14th* day of Adar
15	Shushan Purim is on the *15th* day of Adar
127	Ahasuerus ruled over *127* provinces
10,000	Haman promised the king *10,000* shekels for the royal treasury after the Jews would be killed

QUIZ QUESTIONS FOR PURIM

QUESTIONS:

ANSWERS:

1. Give the Hebrew day and month of Purim.
2. The Fast of Esther is observed:
   a) on the day before Purim
   b) on the day of Purim
   c) on the day after Purim
3. By what name is the day after Purim called?
4. Of what does Shushan Purim remind us?

5. How many times is the Megilla read on Purim? And when?
6. Why is noise made whenever Haman's name is mentioned during the Megilla reading?
7. What is the *Al Ha-Nisim*?
8. What is the favorite food for Purim?
9. a) What is the Seudah?
   b) When is it eaten?
10. What is meant by *Mishloach Manot*?
11. Name a favorite form of merrymaking practiced on Purim.
12. What is meant by *Purim Spielers*?

1. 14th day of Adar
2. a) On the day before Purim

3. Shushan Purim

4. Of the fact that the Jews of Shushan could not observe Purim until the 15th day of Adar, since on the 14th they were busy fighting to save themselves from the Persians
5. Twice, during the evening and the following morning
6. Because Haman was descended from Amalekites, a people who once attacked the Israelites in a very cowardly manner
7. One of the special prayers recited on Purim
8. Hammentash
9. a) The main Purim meal
   b) Toward the late afternoon or early evening on Purim day
10. The sending of gifts to one another
11. Masquerading
12. Purim actors who went around giving plays on Purim

101

13. The story of Purim took place in which of the following countries:
    a) Israel
    b) Egypt
    c) Persia
    d) Babylonia

    13. c) Persia

14. Name the capital city of Persia that is mentioned in the Purim story.

    14. Shushan

15. Who was Ahasuerus?

    15. King of Persia

16. Ahasuerus' first queen was:
    a) Esther
    b) Vashti
    c) Zeresh

    16. b) Vashti

17. What did the King offer to give to Esther?

    17. Half of his Kingdom

Adloyada, the Purim carnival in Tel Aviv.
(Courtesy Israel Information Services.)

18. What is the meaning of the Hebrew word *Pur?*
18. A lot, or a chance

19. Why is Purim called the Feast of Lots?
19. Because Haman cast lots to decide the month and the day on which to kill the Jews

20. Why did Haman want to kill the Jews?
20. Because Mordecai the Jew wouldn't bow down to him

21. Why is the following sentence incorrect? Ahasuerus chose Esther as Queen because she was Jewish.
21. Because Esther did not tell the King that she was a Jewess

22. Why did Esther at first hesitate to go before the King?
22. Because she wasn't allowed to see him uninvited, and the penalty was death

23. Who was Mordecai?
23. Esther's cousin who helped save the Jews

24. a) Why was Mordecai honored by the King?
    b) How was he honored?
    c) Who decided how he was to be honored?
24. a) Because he had saved the King's life by reporting the plot of the two guards
    b) By being paraded through the streets of Shushan
    c) Haman, who thought that he himself was to be honored

25. What were the two guards, whom Mordecai overheard, plotting to do?
25. To kill the King

26. What did Mordecai refuse to do for Haman?
26. To bow down to him

27. In the parade through Shushan, who rode and who led the horse?
27. Mordecai rode and Haman led the horse

28. In which book of the Bible is the story of Purim to be found?
28. In the Book of Esther

29. a) What are the Megillot?
    b) How many of them are there in the Bible?
29. a) Five short Books of the Bible which are read on certain festivals and holy days
    b) Five

30. How does the Book of Esther differ from all other Books of the Bible?
30. The name of God is not mentioned there

103

31. Why do we observe the Fast of Esther?	31. To remind us of how Esther and her maidens as well as other Jews fasted before she went to see the King
32. Why is the Hammentash shaped like a triangle?	32. To remind us of the shape of Haman's hat
33. Name at least one lesson to be learned from the Story of Purim.	33. a) Not to depend too much upon the good will of any wordly ruler b) Never to give up hope in the face of even the greatest danger
34. Which American festival is similar to Purim in the way it is observed?	34. Thanksgiving Day
35. What was a *Shalach Monos Tragger?*	35. The man who carried Purim gifts from house to house
36. From which people was Haman descended?	36. The Amalekites
37. Why did Haman choose the month of Adar for killing the Jews?	37. There were no Jewish festivals or other important days for the Jews during that month at that time
38. Queen Esther had another name. What was it?	38. Hadassah
39. Name the Hebrew tribe from which Mordecai was descended.	39. The tribe of Benjamin
40. What is the *Adloyadah?*	40. The official Purim festival celebration of Israel
41. What did Haman promise the King if all the Jews would be killed?	41. A large sum of money to be taken from the Jews, for the Royal Treasury
42. How were the Jews finally saved?	42. They fought off their attackers with weapons the King had given them

PESAH

One of the oldest, most dramatic and most colorful of all our festivals is Passover. Observed for thousands of years, it is familiar to almost everyone. Yet much remains that is either not known or known very little.

As with the previous holidays so here too we present in a very general way the reasons WHY we observe Passover and some ways of HOW to observe it. In addition, you will no doubt find the "Terms" and "Numbers" to be very useful.

In some ways Passover is perhaps the most difficult of all our festivals to observe, due to its many laws and regulations, especially with respect to the food we eat during these eight days. There is a valid reason for each of these laws. To understand these properly requires some Jewish knowledge and background.

That is why a selected list of references has been provided. Also, Biblical references have been inserted within the reading material itself. Be sure to look these up in your Bible. They will tell you a great deal and bring you closer to the original sources of Jewish learning and civilization.

HAPPY PESAH! HAG SAMEACH!

WHY WE OBSERVE PASSOVER

Z'man Heruteynu is a familiar name by which the festival of Passover is known. It means: The season of our freedom. How did it get this name? What kind of freedom was attained? The best answers to these questions will be found in the events leading up to the first Passover. Let us examine them briefly.

The earliest promise of freedom for Israel was the one made by God to Abraham, the first Hebrew. When the Lord spoke to Abraham He promised him that his descendants would some day "be a stranger in a land that is not theirs and (their masters) shall cause them to suffer for four hundred years . . . . . the nation whom they shall serve will I judge (that is, punish); and afterward shall they (the Hebrews) come out with great wealth" (Genesis, 15:13).

The events that followed as told in Exodus, Chapters I-XIII, bear out God's words to Abraham. At the invitation of Joseph (Jacob's favorite son, who was second to the King of Egypt) Jacob with his sons and their families (70 in all) settled in Egypt. Years later, under another king, when Jacob's descendants had grown very mighty in numbers, they were made slaves and suffered severe persecution. Finally, under the leadership of Moses and Aaron, they became free, but only after ten plagues had been brought upon the Egyptians.

Just as the Hebrews were departing from Egypt, two important events took place. First, on the night before the Exodus, the Israelites were commanded to slaughter a lamb and sprinkle its blood on the doorposts of their houses as a sign for the Angel of Death to pass over the Jewish homes. This ceremony later became part of the Temple offering on Passover.

Then, as they were preparing dough to bake bread for their journey, they were urged to make great haste; the dough did not rise but stayed flat and became the first matzot. This too turned into one of the most important Passover observances. The explanation is included in the HOW section.

For the Israelites this freedom meant not only the end of their slavery but also the beginning of the Jewish nation. From now on they would be not just twelve loosely-organized tribes, but a nation under God. In fact, the month in which they left Egypt (the Hebrew month of Nissan) was now designated as the first month of the year. Nissan therefore became the "head of the months" (Exodus 12:2).

However, in addition to the historical reason just mentioned, Passover is also observed for an agricultural reason. This festival marked the beginning of the grain season. (We will find that two other festivals—Shavuot and Sukkot—are also observed for these two general reasons.)

Now, the freedom which the Israelites won by leaving Egypt had a much broader meaning and greater significance for them than merely the freedom of one single nation. For a nation to fight against its rulers and win its independence was nothing new or unusual in the history of mankind. But for a people to become free and independent for a special purpose and a unique mission—that was something out of the ordinary.

As for the Israelites, the Exodus from Egypt had a double purpose. For them it meant, first, ending the centuries of untold suffering and crushing slavery; and, secondly, becoming a nation not by fighting for their freedom, but by living under the laws of God, thanks to Whom they had won that freedom.

But even this was not enough. It was the destiny of the Israelites not to enjoy their freedom unless it also set an example for other nations to follow. World history since the Exodus proves how true this has been; we can see how other peoples were inspired by Israel's shining example. The history of the Jews is filled with endless tales of our struggle in defense of freedom for all peoples everywhere. For the Jew felt that no man has a right to make a slave of any man, because all of us were equally created in God's image. It is therefore the right of every man to develop himself to his maximum capacities and to make of himself whatever he wishes.

This, then, is the underlying thought that guides us as we celebrate this lovely and happy freedom festival of Passover. But freedom is of little value unless it is wisely used. Passover inspires us anew to put into practice the freedom which our Israelite ancestors achieved after they were delivered from Egypt. So important and meaningful has this historic event been in the life of our people that the phrase "remembering the Exodus from Egypt" appears quite frequently in our prayers, in numerous places in the Torah and in other Jewish literature.

The HOW section tells about the laws of Passover which help make it a genuine pleasure to celebrate this holiday.

THE HOW OF OBSERVING PASSOVER

Did you ever realize that when you observe Passover you are actually "living through history"? This means that you, along with your fellow-Jews the world over, are doing some of the same things that our forefathers did a few thousand years ago, and that our people have been doing ever since. When you follow the laws of Passover, you are not merely a spectator watching a show, you yourself are a participant. It is, therefore, most essential that you first learn how to participate in this festival properly. To this end we will now explain briefly some of the most important ceremonies for Passover.

Passover has another familiar name, *Hag Ha-Matzot* (the feast of unleavened bread). Because the Israelites had to let their dough bake as flat cakes (matzot) instead of bread, all forms of bread and other foods containing leaven are forbidden on Passover. This means that only specially-prepared Passover foods are allowed during this eight-day festival.

This, in turn, requires the use of special dishes, utensils, linens, etc. for those special foods. It thus becomes necessary to make careful house-cleaning preparations weeks beforehand. The entire house must be thoroughly cleaned in order to usher in the Passover properly, so that no leaven, or hametz, will remain there. All these preparations are climaxed by a special ceremony on the night before Passover, when the house is searched for hametz, which is then burned the following morning. (The description and blessing for this ceremony may be found on the first page or two of most Haggadahs.)

The eight days of Passover are divided as follows: The first two and the last two days are observed as a major festival when no work is permitted. During the middle four days, known as *Hol Ha-Moed* (the half-holiday), work is permitted (except on the Sabbath) but most of the other laws of Passover still apply.

On the first two nights of Passover a special service, known as a "seder" (order), is held at home when much of the story of Passover is read and explained with the aid of certain objects in readiness on the table. The seder service usually appeals to children as they have a prominent part in it and enjoy the excitement, fun, stories, songs, etc. connected with it.

The object of the seder is two-fold. First, we recall the Pascal Lamb feast mentioned in the Bible (Exodus, chapter 12) and secondly, we retell the story of Passover in an interesting and meaningful manner. For this reason, a special book known as a "Haggadah" is used during the service. The term "Haggadah" means "telling" and is based on the commandment

Passover plate, Italy.

ROASTED EGG   ROASTED BONE
         BITTER HERBS
GREEN   BROWN
  VEGETABLE   MIXTURE
         LETTUCE

✳✳✳

in Exodus 13:8, *V'higadta L'vincha* (and you shall tell your son), when he asks the reason for these laws and commandments. In fact, this commandment also prompts the child's asking the "Four Questions," so that the telling of the story of the Exodus may come in response to his questions. (See also Deuteronomy 6:20.)

Among the objects on the table during the seder service are matzot, wine, a seder plate, and salt water. The seder plate contains the bitter herbs, the roasted egg, the roasted bone, the brown mixture called *Harosset*, and green vegetables. Most of these foods are tasted as the seder progresses and they become a living reminder of the story of Passover. For example, the bitterness of the *maror* (horseradish) calls to mind the bitterness of the slavery our ancestors had to endure in Egypt.

All in all, there are fifteen parts to the seder service for each of the two nights. The Passover meal is one of these. However, the more serious portion of the seder comes before the meal. The last few portions thereafter are mostly songs, hymns, etc.

One of the highlights of the seder is the asking of the Four Questions by one of the younger children. The father's answers to these questions then become the greater part of the story of Passover, including the "returning" of the *afikoman* matza, among other things. There is much more to the seder service which can be found in any traditional Haggadah. Read one through carefully to see for yourself.

As Passover is a major festival, no work is permitted and the synagogue services are a bit longer than usual, due to additional prayers and Torah readings. During Hol Ha-Moed (the middle four days) work is permitted, but the festival spirit still remains. Many of the prayers and Torah readings are continued from the first two days.

The last two days of Passover (like the first two) are again full holidays. On the seventh day the story of the miracle of the Red Sea is read in the Torah, since this is the day when it is said to have occurred. Finally, on the eighth day we recite the "Yizkor" prayer, in memory of the departed. This prayer is usually postponed for the closing day of a festival to prevent having the holiday joy saddened by saying it earlier.

We trust that by now you realize the many ways that Passover brings both gladness and meaning to the Jew as he celebrates his ancestors' winning their freedom. This is the function of every ceremony mentioned so far. Each one of these observances is meant to add to the dignity and feeling with which Passover should fill every Jewish heart. For example, when a Jewish father sits at his seder table, with comfortable cushions to lean on, he is there as the traditional king with his wife as his queen and the children as his princes and princesses.

But, in addition, Passover also reminds him of his past (Israel's exodus), his present (sharing his freedom with others), and his future (keeping this lesson alive for all coming generations). It behooves us, therefore, to remember that simply talking and reading about Passover is not enough. It must be observed and made a joyful experience in our personal lives both as Jews and as members of society. This makes you a better, happier Jew.

TERMS FOR PASSOVER

A-FI-KO-MAN	"Dessert," or the "hidden matza," eaten just before the Grace after Meals is said
A-HA-RON SHEL PESAH	The eighth and last day of Passover
B'DI-KAT HA-METZ	Searching for unleavened bread on the night before Passover
BITTER HERBS	Usually, bitter horseradish, which is tasted during the seder service
BIUR HA-METZ	Burning the Hametz which was found the night before Passover
COUNTING OF THE OMER	The ceremony of counting the number of weeks and days between Passover and Shavuot
EREV PESAH	The Eve of Passover, or the day before Passover
EXODUS	The departure of the Israelites from Egypt under Moses
FOUR QUESTIONS	The questions asked by the youngest child during the early part of the seder service
FOUR SONS	The four types of sons described in the Haggadah
HAD GADYA	"The Only Kid," a favorite seder hymn
HAGGADAH	The special booklet containing the seder service
HAG HA-MATZOT	"Feast of Unleavened Bread" (Matzot)—another name for Passover
HAG HA-PESAH	Hebrew for "Festival of Passover"
HA-METZ	Food that we are forbidden to eat on Passover
HA-RO-SSET	The brown mixture, usually made of apples, cinnamon, nuts and wine and tasted during the seder service
HOL HA-MO-ED	The middle four days of Passover when some work is permitted
KARPASS	The green vegetable (or potato) found on the seder plate
K'ORAH	The Hebrew word for the "seder plate"

KOS SHEL ELIYAHU	The Cup of Elijah which stands undrunk during the entire seder service
MAH NISH-TA-NAH	Beginning words from the "Four Questions" (Hebrew)
MA-OT HIT-TIM	The special Matzot Fund which is used to help needy Jews before Passover
MAROR	Hebrew for "bitter herbs"
MAT-ZA	Hebrew for "unleavened bread"
MO-A-DIM L'SIM'HAH	"Festivals of Joy," a festival greeting
NISSAN	The first month of the Hebrew calendar, the one when the Exodus from Egypt took place
OMER	The measure of barley brought to the Temple during the seven weeks between Passover and Shavuot
PASCAL LAMB	The special lamb-offering for Passover
SEDER	A home ceremony held on the first two nights of Passover (one in Israel)
SEDER PLATE	The special plate containing some of the symbols for the seder service
S'FIRAH	Hebrew for "Counting of the Omer"
SHABBAT HA-GA-DOL	"The Great Sabbath", the Sabbath before Passover
SHALOSH REGA-LIM	"The Three Festivals" of Pilgrimage: Passover, Shavuot and Sukkot
SHIR HA-SHI-RIM	Hebrew for Song of Songs
SH'VI-I SHEL PESAH	The seventh day of Passover, which is the first of the two final days
SONG OF SONGS	The special megilla read on Passover
TEN PLAGUES	The ten forms of punishment with which the Egyptians were smitten just before the Israelites left Egypt
UNLEAVENED BREAD	Matzot which the Israelites baked as they left Egypt
YIZKOR	The memorial prayer recited on the last day of most festivals

Z'MAN HE-RU-TEY-NU	"Season of Our Freedom," another name for Passover
Z'RO-AH	The roasted bone (or meat) found on the seder plate

NUMBERS TO REMEMBER FOR PASSOVER

1	Nissan, the month when Passover is celebrated, is the *first* month of the year In Israel only *one* seder is conducted
2	The seder service is held on the first *two* nights of Passover (except in Israel) *Two* blessings are recited for the matzo during the seder You wash your hands *twice* during the seder
3	Three *matzot* are used during the seder Passover is one of the *three* pilgrimage festivals
4	*Four* cups of wine are drunk during the Haggadah reading at the seder *Four* sons are described in the Haggadah *Four* days of Hol Ha-Moed
7	On the *seventh* day of Passover, the miracle of the Red Sea occurred *Seven* weeks is the period required for Counting of the Omer
8	Passover lasts *eight* days Yizkor is recited on the *eighth* day of Passover
10	The *Ten* Plagues preceded the Israelites' exodus from Egypt
15	There are *fifteen* parts to the seder service
40	The Israelites wandered in the desert for *forty* years
70	When Jacob and his family settled in Egypt they totalled *seventy* souls
600,000	When the Israelites left Egypt they had 600,000 men of fighting age

QUIZ QUESTIONS FOR PASSOVER

QUESTIONS:

1. What is the Hebrew date for Passover?
2. How many days is Pesah celebrated?
3. To which group of festivals does Pesah belong?
4. How did Passover get its name?
5. Passover is celebrated because . . .
6. Give three additional names for the Festival of Passover.
7. What is the most important idea connected with Pesah?
8. What is meant by Hol Ha-Moed?
9. The Sabbath before Passover is known by what name?
10. What is the name of the day before Pesah?
11. a) On which night of Pesah do we begin counting the Omer (S'firah)?
    b) For how many days is the Omer counted?

ANSWERS:

1. 15th through the 22nd of Nissan
2. Eight days
3. Shalosh Regalim, the three pilgrimage festivals
4. Because the angel of death *passed over* (Pesah in Hebrew) the houses of the Israelites and did not slay their first-born
5. The children of Israel were freed from slavery in Egypt
6. a) Hag Ha-Aviv (Festival of Spring)
   b) Hag Ha-Matzot (Festival of Matzot)
   c) Z'man He-ruteynu (Festival of our Freedom)
7. Freedom
8. The four middle days of Passover when some of the laws of the first two and the last two days do not apply
9. *Shabbat Ha-Gadol* (The Great Sabbath)
10. Erev Pesah
11. a) The second night
    b) For 49 days, or seven weeks

12. On which nights of Pesah is a seder conducted:
    a) Outside Israel?
    b) In Israel?
13. a) What is the "Yizkor service"?
    b) On which day of Pesah is it recited?
14. a) What is meant by *Hametz?*
    b) Why do we sell the Hametz before Passover?

12. a) The first *two* nights
    b) The first night

13. a) Memorial prayer for the departed
    b) The last (8th) day

14. a) Food that is forbidden during Passover
    b) To follow the law which forbids our seeing, having or owning any Hametz

Pilgrimage to Mount Zion on Passover.

15. Name three or more steps in preparing for Pesah.	15. Changing the dishes; buying matzot; selling the hametz; giving Maot Hittim; burning the hametz
16. How is Pesah observed in the home?	16. By conducting a seder; eating matzot; using special dishes during Pesah; and other festival observances
17. Why do we eat matzot during Pesah?	17. To remind us of the haste in which the Israelites left Egypt when their dough turned into flat cakes or matzot
18. Name the special book used for the seder.	18. Haggadah
19. Name three things we do at the seder service.	19. Recite the Kiddush; ask questions (Mah Nishtanah); drink four cups of wine; open the door for Elijah; hide and then eat the *afikoman;* sing *Had Gadya* and other songs
20. What objects are placed on the seder plate?	20. Roasted bone or meat; roasted egg; *Harosset* (brown mixture); green vegetables; bitter herbs
21. Why do we drink four cups of wine during the seder?	21. To recall the four promises which God made to the Israelites
22. What is the *Kos Eliyahu?*	22. A large cup of wine which stands (undrunk) in honor of Elijah, the prophet
23. During the seder, why do we eat the *maror* (bitter herbs)?	23. To remind us of the bitter times the ancient Israelites suffered while in Egypt
24. What does the *z'roah* (roasted bone or meat) represent?	24. The Pascal Lamb which was offered as a special sacrifice during Temple days
25. a) What is the *afikoman?* b) What is done with it during the seder service?	25. a) The part of the middle matza used for "dessert" b) We first hide it; then we eat it at the end of the meal

26. Which book of the Bible, written by King Solomon, is read on Passover?	26. The Megilla of Shir Ha-Shirim (Song of Songs)
27. The story of Pesah is found in which book of the Torah?	27. *Shmot* (Exodus)
28. Which of the following do we use on Pesah? *Hakafot, Harosset* or *Kapparot*	28. Harosset
29. What is the *Maot Hittim*?	29. A Fund collected before Pesah for helping to provide needy Jews with matzot and other Pesah needs
30. Which of the following is the correct Passover greeting? *L'shanah tovah; Hag sameach; Shabbat shalom; Moadim L'Simhah*	30. Hag sameach or Moadim L'Simhah
31. Why do we eat the *afikoman*?	31. So that the meal may begin and end with matzot
32. What is the difference between *B'dikat Hametz* and *Biur Hametz*?	32. B'dikat Hametz—Searching for Hametz Biur Hametz—Burning the Hametz

Jews from the Arabian desert (Hadramaut) celebrating the seder in Israel where they now live.
(Courtesy Keren Hayesod.)

33. By what time must the Hametz be burned?
34. What is the *Had Gadya?*
35. What is the Hebrew name for the seder plate?
36. What is the agricultural reason for observing Pesah?
37. Name the four sons mentioned in the Haggadah.
38. Which familiar story is read from the Torah on the seventh day of Passover?
39. Give the Hebrew names for the 7th and 8th days of Passover.
40. a) During the Seder what is done as the Ten Plagues are read?
    b) Why?

41. a) On what does the master of the house sit during the seder?
    b) Why?

33. By around 10:000 A.M. of the morning before Pesah
34. A well-known song sung at the close of the seder service
35. *K'orah*
36. It is the beginning of the grain or barley season
37. The wise son; the wicked son; the simple son; and the one who does not know how to ask a question
38. The miracle of the Red Sea
39. Seventh—*Shvii Shel Pesah*
    Eighth—*Aharon Shel Pesah*
40. a) One drop of wine is poured out for each plague and one for the initial letter of each word
    b) To show sorrow for the Egyptians' suffering during the plagues
41. a) On pillows
    b) As a symbol of freedom (Every Jew is a "king" on this night)

ISRAEL INDEPENDENCE DAY

Yom Ha'Atzmaut, Israel's Independence Day, is only a 'youngster' compared to all the older festivals but it is fast gaining in popularity. Before long it too will become the equal of its sister-festivals. As you will soon find out, certain religious observances are also being attached to it.

To help summarize and better understand the many historical events mentioned in the WHY section, a special table called "A Time-Table of a Two Thousand Year Struggle" has been included. Refer to this table and return to the reading portions as often as necessary.

Helpful to your understanding and remembering are the "Terms" and the "Numbers" we have included. If you share them with your family and friends they too will learn and thus enjoy the great day all the more.

As always, the material listed under "For Further Reading" comprises books, reference works, pamphlets, and the like. If you read as many of these as you can, they will deepen your knowledge and appreciation of the significance of this historic holiday.

We Jews, as you may already know, have a long and colorful history behind us. The second half of that history (about 2,000 years) is largely covered by the events discussed in the WHY section. Reading some of the history texts listed under "For Further Reading" will give you a good idea of how the Jewish people has traveled the long road of the past two thousand years and what it was that made it possible for us to continue as Jews.

HAPPY YOM HA'ATZMAUT!

THE WHY OF ISRAEL'S INDEPENDENCE DAY

As the fourth of July is an American holiday because it marks the independence of the thirteen colonies (which then became the first 13 of the United States) from Great Britain, so the 5th of Iyar, 5708 (corresponding to May 14, 1948) is Israel's Independence Day—a great Jewish holiday, because on that day the present State of Israel was born. But this event means even more to Jews than the birth of independence does to other nations because now for the first time in nearly 2,000 years, our people has a land of its own and is an independent nation once more.

However, in order to understand how this historic event came about seemingly so suddenly and so quickly, we need to know the story of our people. Thus we will see that the struggle for Jewish independence, which had failed at the time of Bar Kochba and Rabbi Akiba when Lag B'Omer originated, finally culminated in the present-day State of Israel. But, since so much has happened between these two periods, let us review these intervening events briefly.

Following Judea's second defeat by Rome the Jews suffered more than ever before. Not only were many of them driven from their land, Israel, to all other parts of the Roman Empire but for those who remained, life in Israel was bitter under the crushing tyranny of the Roman rulers.

Nevertheless, in spirit the Jews were not defeated. Wherever they lived they studied the Torah diligently and created such famous works as the Talmud (the Oral Law) and other sacred writings.

During the Middle Ages (or the "Dark Ages") when human suffering was widespread due to wars, ignorance, superstition, etc., the Jews still clung to their study of Torah. Not for a moment did they lose hope for a rebuilt Israel, even though they had been exiled from three major countries (England, 1290; France, 1394; and Spain, 1492). Because of these and other explanations, the Jew became known as the "Wandering Jew" without a home or a land of his own. In fact, during these dark centuries most Jews were forced to live in ghettos, were not allowed to earn a livelihood as they chose, and were frequently humiliated, attacked, robbed, murdered and persecuted in countless other ways.

But all the suffering and persecution could not discourage the Jews from Torah study. Nor did they ever forget their homeland, Israel. Three times a day they prayed for it. Ceaselessly they continued to study the holy books written there. Many Jews also managed to visit or even to settle in Israel. In brief, Israel was always close to their hearts.

*The Israeli Navy parading on Independence Day.
(Courtesy Israel Information Services.)*

When the Dark Ages ended, and liberty and enlightenment began to spread under the influence of the American and French Revolutions, new nations came into being. The Jews thought the time had come for them too to have a land of their own. During the early 19th century, many Hebrew writers as Peretz, Mapu, Smolenskin, Hess, and others, began to encourage the Jews to build up their Land of Israel as a national Jewish homeland. However, it was only near the end of the 19th century (in the 1880's) that greater masses of Jews (chiefly the victims of the Russian persecutions) began to immigrate to Israel and to build the earliest settlements there. You may well imagine the dreadful conditions these earliest *Halutzim* (pioneers) found there: a land long neglected, its soil uncultivated, swamps, deserts, and to top it all—unfriendly Arabs.

Yet these hardy pioneers were not discouraged in the least. Determined to succeed no matter what the sacrifice, they went ahead, draining the swamps, tilling and enriching the soil, and building village after village. Before very long, a number of settlements had sprung up. The best known of these earliest settlements was Rishon L'Tzion.

Even though Israel was then, and for centuries had been, under Ottoman rule as part of the Turkish Empire—by the latter part of the 19th century, as more and more Jews migrated to Israel, while the land was developing and being built up, the Jews of the world now sensed that the time had come for all Jews to organize and turn this ancient land of the Jews into the modern Jewish homeland. This conviction led to the birth of the Zionist movement.

Theodor Herzl, an Austrian-Jewish journalist, was the most influential and famous leader of this movement. He set up the first World Zionist Congress which met in Basle, Switzerland, in 1897. It has been meeting regularly every four years ever since. This Congress, composed of representatives of Jewish communities all over the world, worked to make Israel the land of the Jews, to be governed by the Jews themselves.

Then, in 1917, while World War I was still being fought, came the celebrated Balfour Declaration (named after Arthur J. Balfour, the British Foreign Secretary) in which Great Britain expressed its intention of making it possible to build up Palestine as a Jewish Homeland.

When the war ended, following the victory of all Allied Powers (United States, Great Britain and France) over the Central Powers (Germany, Austria and Turkey) Palestine came under the rule of Great Britain, which had been given the "mandate" to govern it. This arrangement meant that the Jews could have some self-government in Palestine, but under the "protection" of Great Britain.

But the Arabs of Palestine were bitterly opposed to this arrangement and as a result constantly harassed the Jews. Thus periodically many bloody riots broke out in Palestine, when bands of Arabs attacked and killed large numbers of Jews. Those of 1921, 1929, and 1936 were among the worst.

However, the Mandate policy showed its greatest weakness during World War II, while Nazi Germany was in power. During those terror filled years of the early 1940's when thousands upon thousands of Jewish refugees from Nazi lands were clamoring to enter Palestine (since most nations, including the United States, refused to admit them) they found the gates of the homeland closed tight against them. Why? Because the British were afraid of Arab objections to having masses of Jews enter

Israeli tankists on maneuver.
(Courtesy Israel Information Services.)

Palestine. Nevertheless, the Israelis did manage to smuggle many long-suffering Jews secretly into the Land.

This British opposition prompted the formation of Jewish underground resistance "armies" who fought both the British and the Arabs. The Haganah ("self-defense"), the Palmach ("commando troops") and Irgun Zvai Leumi ("Jewish National Army") were among the best-known early resistance movements.

In addition to those and other efforts, many Jews now realized that Jews could have security only as an independent Jewish nation, and they concentrated all efforts on a political battle aimed at this end. Finally, on November 29, 1947, the United Nations voted to have Great Britain give up its mandate rule of Palestine in order to allow it to become a full, independent nation on its own. *This act gave birth to the State of Israel. It was born on May 14, 1948*, thus becoming a free and sovereign nation, after its people had been scattered and homeless for nearly 2,000 years.

However, Palestine had been divided by the U.N. decision into two sections, separate Israeli and Arab territories. As a result, the area of the new State of Israel amounted to about one-eighth of what it had been during Biblical times. But most of the Jews did not object, as long as the tiny territory was now their own.

Dr. Chaim Weizmann, an outstanding Zionist leader for many years—and a former professor of chemistry at England's University of Manchester—who had been chiefly instrumental in having the Balfour Declaration issued, became the State of Israel's First President.

Naturally, since many Arabs had always been opposed to a Jewish state, they immediately went to war against the newly-born Israel. But the Jewish army was ready for them. With superhuman courage they fought off the armies of seven Arab countries. Within less than a year the Arab nations all signed an armistice with Israel, thus ending Israel's War of Liberation.* However, attacks by smaller Arab armies still persisted.

Now, the State of Israel could settle down to the task of building up the land, the nation, the government and world relations. As a result, within a few years, Israel had already become the leading country of the Middle East. It was fully recognized as a sovereign state and admitted to the United Nations in 1949.

This, in short, is the story of the birth of the State of Israel. You can see what a long, hard struggle it has been. Therefore, every year, on the 5th of the month of Iyar, as Israel's Independence Day is being observed, Jews everywhere realize what it is that she is celebrating.

Thus, young as this festival is, it has a long, proud and colorful history behind it. Unlike all other Jewish festivals, Israel's Independence Day is observed not for something that happened a long time ago, but for a recent event that has been nearly 2,000 years in coming.

Also, it is a source of joy to us that an event of such significance with such a long history, took place within our own time. In other words, you yourself are living in a period when extraordinary history is actually being made by our people.

Nevertheless, we Jews feel that being an independent nation, in a land of our own, is only the beginning of a brighter future for our people. At the same time, we must not forget or overlook the vast problems and difficulties which confront the State of Israel. Perhaps the greatest of these is Israel's military security. Twice since the War of Liberation of 1949—

---

* But this end of the war did not mean that the Arab nations now recognized the State of Israel. It only meant that fighting was being suspended for the time being. In fact, even to this day, the Arabs still consider themselves to be at war with Israel and they still refuse to recognize her independence.

Independence Day Parade, Jerusalem.

first during the Sinai Campaign in 1956, and later in the heroic Six-Day War of 1967—Israel succeeded in defending itself against a savage enemy, which outnumbered the State 40 to 1.

Numerous other problems also demand immediate attention, such as: settling those who come from nearly all parts of the world; building up industries and agriculture; keeping the workers employed; providing for the education and health of all, etc.

But, the Israelis have never despaired in the face of any crisis. We may therefore expect that all the pressing problems will find a solution and that Israel will show the world the way to a democratic, peaceful and righteous life.

From all this you now have a much clearer picture of the long, arduous and adventurous road that began with the original Lag B'Omer and continued to modern Israel's Independence Day. Both festivals tell a story of the Jew's struggle to survive and to carry his message to the world. This struggle shows how the Jew has refused to die, chiefly because he has had something to live for; his Torah together with other spiritual treasures of 4,000 years of unbroken tradition.

TIME-TABLE OF A 2,000 YEAR STRUGGLE
FROM ROMAN RULE TO INDEPENDENCE

(B.C.E.—Before The Common Era   C.E.—Common Era, same as "A.D.")

63 B.C.E.	Pompey conquers Judea. Beginning of Roman Rule. End of Jewish Independence.
70 C.E.	Judea loses war to Rome. Temple destroyed. Great Exile begins.
135 C.E.	Second war with Rome. Exile and persecution by the Romans. Torah study continues on.
MIDDLE AGES (500-1500)	Persecution, ghettos, expulsions (England, 1290, France, 1394; Spain, 1492). Jews still remember Torah and Israel.
NEW FREEDOM (1776-1789)	Nationalism. Freedom, equality for all. Jews also want and demand equal rights.
1800-1850	New nations are born. Jews also want to be a nation, like all other nations. Famous Hebrew writers: Hess, Peretz, Smolenskin, Mapu, Pinsker, etc.
1880-1920	Earliest modern-day settlements in Israel. Aliyot. Halutzim. Beginning of Zionism (Herzl).
1897	First World Zionist Congress, Basle, Switzerland.
1914-1918	World War I. Britain favors Zionism. General Allenby captures Jerusalem, 1918.
1917	Balfour Declaration. Chaim Weizmann.
1920	British Mandatory Government begins. Jewish self-government. Arab riots.
1933-1945	Nazi refugees struggle to enter Palestine. Rise of Jewish underground defense armies: Haganah, Irgun Zvai Leumi, and others.
1947	United Nations approves establishment of separate Arab and Jewish independent states in Palestine.
May 14, 1948	Birth of the State of Israel. Arabs attack Israel. Israel's War of Liberation.
1949	Arab-Israeli Armistice agreements. Israed admitted to United Nations.
1956	Sinai Campaign.
1967	Six-Day War.
1973	Yom Kippur War.

HOW ISRAEL'S INDEPENDENCE DAY IS CELEBRATED

Since this festival is still very new and young compared to all our other holidays it does not as yet have as many customs and traditions as have our older festivals. Nevertheless, Jews the world over are finding more and more ways of observing it. Naturally, most celebrations of Israel's Independence Day are held in Israel. However, Jews throughout the world also join in celebrating it in one way or another. Some of these observances will now be described.

In the State of Israel, Independence Day is marked by joy and merrymaking because of the deep pride and love the Israelis feel for their country. But the gaiety is accompanied by a feeling of sadness and by the memory of those who fell in the bloody struggle for Israel's freedom. Our people had to pay a high price indeed for liberty.

Therefore, the day before *Yom Ha'Atzmaut* (the Hebrew Independence Day) is *Yom Ha-Zikaron* (Memorial Day). Immediately after sundown of the preceding day—for all Jewish festivals begin on the preceding evening—a siren is sounded and all activity suddenly stops. Everything is closed and silent, including all cafes, theatres, and all other places of entertainment. That evening sorrow prevails as everyone calls to mind the dead heroes of Israel's wars. The following day is devoted to visiting the cemeteries to decorate and pray at the graves of the dead.

But, at the end of that day, at the blast of another siren, the entire nation plunges into merrymaking and celebration. In many homes the *Hallel* prayer is recited, followed by a festive dinner. Throughout the land carnivals, dancing, singing, etc. are in order. The next day tens of thousand of Israelis flock to witness the grand military parade, when units of Israel's army, navy and air force march smartly in formation and display the latest tanks, planes and other war equipment that is part of Israel's military might. Recently, however, the Israelis have been conducting discussions whether to continue such military parades, or to introduce other ways of officially celebrating Yom Ha'Atzmaut.

Connected with Independence Day is another custom that is fast becoming an Israeli tradition: the international Bible Quiz. Although the final contest of this typically Israeli event actually takes place shortly before Independence Day, it is usually associated with the latter. Bible Quiz winners from all over the world meet in Jerusalem for the final contest. Glued to their radios, the entire nation listens intently to these contestants, just as do World Series fans in America. (In other words, it may be said that the final Bible Quiz is to Israel what the World Series is to the U.S.A.)

During Temple Days, the Jews went on a pilgrimage to Jerusalem three times a year (on Passover, Shavuot, and Sukkot). In the same spirit many groups of Israelis go on a three-day hike to Jerusalem. Walking instead of riding, they average about fifteen to twenty miles per day, singing as they go, camping overnight on the way.

In short, Independence Day in Israel is observed in a variety of ways. In time, no doubt, other manners of observance will be added, some of which will become established traditions.

While Yom Ha'Atzmaut is not as widely celebrated in America as it is in Israel, even here it is developing into an established holiday. Many American Jews celebrate and honor it by taking a trip to Israel and sharing in the celebration with the Israelis. The number of such American Jewish visitors increases from year to year.

On this day the Israeli Embassy in Washington, as well as all the consulates of the State of Israel located throughout the United States, observe open house for all visitors. Many Jewish schools and organizations visit these institutions in large groups and thus become better acquainted with what Israel is doing.

Even though Israel's Independence Day is not a religious festival, many synagogues do observe it with special services which include the reading of special Biblical portions in addition to the regular prayers. These religious observances are also becoming more and more popular.

In most Jewish schools, Yom Ha'Atzmaut programs are regularly scheduled. They consist of assemblies, dramatic programs, visits to places connected with Israel, and the like. Other Jewish organizations and institutions in growing numbers likewise observe it with a special program in honor of this day.

It has also become customary for many American cities to schedule large parades in observance of Israel's Independence Day. The best-known and most colorful of these parades is the one held in New York, where many thousands of Jews line both sides of Fifth Avenue to cheer the numerous groups of marchers and the colorful floats depicting Israel's history and progress. Most Jewish organizations and schools take part in these parades.

Here we have mentioned only a few of the many forms of observing Israel's Independence Day. As Israel grows and as more and more Jews work for Israel's welfare, it is to be expected that additional observances will be introduced. However, no matter what the form in which this young festival is celebrated, the feeling of every Jew is not only the pride in his homeland, but also a realization that Israel faces many pressing problems and therefore needs the help of every loyal Jew. Israel is the homeland of all Jews. In other words, the Land of Israel cannot be separated from the People of Israel.

NAMES AND TERMS FOR ISRAEL'S INDEPENDENCE DAY

BALFOUR, ARTHUR J.	The British foreign secretary after whom the "Balfour Declaration" was named
BALFOUR DECLARATION	A declaration issued through Lord Balfour, of Great Britain, expressing her intention of helping the Jews to make Palestine a Jewish homeland
BASLE	The Swiss city where the first World Zionist Congress took place in 1897
BIBLE QUIZ	The final round of this famous Bible contest, when contestants from all over the world gather in Jerusalem, a few days prior to Independence Day
ENGLAND	Jews were expelled from there in 1290
FRANCE	Jews were expelled from there in 1394
GHETTOS	The part of a city where many Jews were forced to live during the Middle Ages
HAGANAH	("Self-defense") One of the Jewish secret self-defense armies of the World War II period
HALLEL	A prayer of thanksgiving recited on joyous festivals
HALUTZ (plural—HALUTZIM)	Israel pioneer
HERZL, THEODOR	One of the famous founders of the Zionist movement
IYAR	The Hebrew month when both Lag B'Omer and Independence Day occur
MANDATE	A form of rule, known as a "protectorate," under which Great Britain, following World War I, gave Palestine some home rule
MEMORIAL DAY	English for Yom Ha-Zikaron
MILITARY SECURITY	The security of being free from military attack as Israel seeks to be
ORAL LAW	The rabbinic law which grew out of a study of the Bible, but which was handed down from teacher to student, from mouth to mouth, or, orally, not in written form

OTTOMAN EMPIRE	Same as Turkish
PALESTINE	The name by which the land of Israel was called prior to the establishment of the State of Israel
PALMACH	"Shock troops," a Jewish self-defense army
RISHON L'TZION	One of the earliest settlements in Israel
SINAI CAMPAIGN	A war fought by Israel against the Arab attackers in the Sinai desert in 1956
SPAIN	Jews were expelled from there in 1492
TALMUD	The Oral Law which grew out of the study of the Torah
THREE-DAY HIKE	The hike taken by Israelis into Jerusalem just before Independence Day
"WANDERING JEW, THE"	A term used regarding the Jews, which was meant to show that they had no land of their own, but were forced to wander all over the earth
WAR OF LIBERATION	The war fought against the Arabs immediately following the birth of the State of Israel
WEIZMANN, CHAIM	First president of the State of Israel
WORLD ZIONIST CONGRESS	A body of representatives of Jews from all over the world, who meet every four years to discuss problems pertaining to Israel
YOM HA'ATZMAUT	Hebrew for "Independence Day"
YOM HA-ZIKARON	Hebrew for "Memorial Day," a day before Independence Day
YOM KIPPUR WAR (1973)	The war fought following a two-front attack by Arabs on Yom Kippur, 1973
ZIONISM	A movement that works for the return of the Jews to the land of Israel, which it seeks to build up as a Jewish homeland

NUMBERS RELATING TO ISRAEL'S INDEPENDENCE DAY

⅛	The area of the State of Israel as of May 14, 1948 was about *one-eighth* of what it was in Biblical times
1	This holiday lasts but *one* day
3	The *three-day* hike which takes place just before Independence Day
5	Yom Ha'Atzmaut falls on the *5th* of Iyar
6	The *Six-Day War* of 1967
14	Israel's first Independence Day was on the *14th* of May
2,000	Nearly *2,000* years have elapsed since the Jewish people lost their independence

SIGNIFICANT DATES TO REMEMBER ON YOM HA'ATZMAUT

1897	1949
1917	1956
1947	1967
1948	1973

QUIZ QUESTIONS—ISRAEL'S INDEPENDENCE DAY

QUESTIONS:

1. a) What is the Hebrew date of Israel's Independence Day?
   b) What was the English date on which it was first observed?

2. Why is it observed?

3. How do we associate Independence Day with Lag B'Omer?

4. What happened to the Jews after their defeat by the Romans?

5. Why didn't the Jews feel lost following the defeat by Rome?

6. What famous Jewish work was produced following the defeat by Rome?

7. From which 3 important countries, and in what years, were the Jews exiled during the Middle Ages?

8. Why was the Jew known during the Middle Ages as the "Wandering Jew"?

9. What made ghetto life so bitter for the Jew during medieval times?

10. How did the Jews keep the land of Israel close to their hearts during the Middle Ages?

ANSWERS:

1. a) 5th day of Iyar
   b) May 14, 1948

2. After nearly 2,000 years, Israel again became an independent nation

3. The fight for freedom that failed them, at the time of Lag B'Omer, was finally won on Independence Day, 1948

4. They were driven out of their land and those who remained in Israel suffered Roman tyranny

5. They continued to study the Torah—and to uphold their faith

6. The Talmud, or the Oral Law

7. England, 1290
   France, 1394
   Spain, 1492

8. Because he had no land of his own and was therefore persecuted and forced to wander from land to land

9. He was often attacked, robbed, shamed and made to suffer in endless ways

10. They prayed for it, read about it, and in some cases even visited there

11. What did many Hebrew writers encourage the Jews to do during the early 19th century?

12. What caused many European Jews to emigrate to Israel during the latter part of the 19th century?

13. What is meant by the term "halutzim"?

14. Name some of the conditions the halutzim found in Israel.

15. What was "Rishon L'Tzion"?

16. What mighty empire of the 19th century and 20th century had ruled Israel for hundreds of years before World War I?

17. a) What is meant by the "Zionist movement"?

   b) When was it born?

18. a) Who was Theodor Herzl?

   b) How did he become famous?

19. a) What was the World Zionist Congress?

   b) When and where did it first take place?
   c) How often does it meet?

11. Build up their land, Israel, and become a nation like all other nations

12. Persecutions, especially in Russia, as well as in other countries

13. Israeli pioneers

14. Deserts, swamps, uncultivated land, and unfriendly Arabs

15. One of the earliest colonies established in Israel

16. The Turkish or Ottoman Empire

17. a) A world organization working to make Israel the national homeland of the Jews
    b) Around the end of the 19th and the beginning of the 20th centuries

18. a) An Austrian journalist who dedicated himself completely to work for Zionism
    b) He organized the First World Zionist Congress, and tried to persuade the nations of the world to agree to make Israel a Jewish homeland

19. a) A body of representatives of Jews from all over the world who wanted to see Israel become a free nation in its own land
    b) In 1897, at Basle, Switzerland
    c) Every four years

20. a) Which nation issued the Balfour Declaration? and when?
    b) What was it?

20. a) Great Britain in 1917
    b) A declaration which stated that Britain favored building Israel up as a Jewish homeland, by and for the Jews, but—under certain conditions

21. What nation ruled Israel immediately after World War I?

21. Great Britain

22. What is meant by "Palestine"?

22. The name of the Land before the rise of the State of Israel

23. What was the "mandate" of Great Britain over Palestine?

23. A political agreement and arrangement by which Britain allowed Palestine to govern itself, although it was under the "protection" of England

24. How did the Arabs of Palestine show their feelings about the mandate after it was declared?

24. They expressed their bitterness toward the Jews by staging a number of riots throughout the land

25. In what way did the mandate policy show its weakness during the 1940's?

25. Britain refused to allow the Jewish refugees from Nazi lands to immigrate to Israel

26. Name a few of the Jewish resistance armies of the World War II period.

26. Haganah; Palmach; Irgun

27. What is so important about November 29, 1947?

27. On that date the United Nations voted to have Great Britain give up its mandate over Palestine and allow Israel to become a fully independent nation on May 14, 1948

28. How did the area of the State of Israel compare with that of Biblical times?

28. It was only about one-eighth as large as it had been in those early days

29. Name the first President of the State of Israel.

29. Chaim Weizmann

30. How long did the War of Liberation last?

30. Less than one year

31. When was Israel admitted to the United Nations?	31. In 1949
32. Independence Day is most different from all our other festivals because (check one) a) It first took place a long time ago. / b) It is a minor and non-religious festival. c) It has a longer history preceding it than any other festival. d) It is the shortest of all our festivals.	32. c) It has a longer (known) history preceding it than any other festival
33. Name one of Israel's major problems today.	33. Military security
34. Name the wars Israel has fought since it became a modern nation.	34. War of Liberation (1948) Sinai Campaign (1956) Six-Day War (1967) Yom Kippur War (1973)
35. Why is it that throughout his history, the Jew has refused to die?	35. Among many other reasons, because he has had something to live for—his Torah, the one greatest source of his life

Another recent festival, one that was born out of the Six-Day War, is "Yom Yerushalayim" (Day of Jerusalem). This special day celebrates the winning back of the entire city of Jerusalem, on the 28th day of Iyar (June 7, 1967), when, for the first time since 70 C.E., the Western Wall and the Temple Mount had returned to Jewish rule, thus unifying the entire city of Jerusalem.

This day is presently observed by reciting special prayers and hymns of thanksgiving in the synagogue. No doubt many other observances and customs will grow out of these few.

NOTE: In connection with the following chapter please refer to SUMMARY AND COMPARISON OF LAG B'OMER AND ISRAEL'S INDEPENDENCE DAY, *page 146.*

LAG B'OMER

Lag B'Omer is not a religious festival (as Rosh HaShana or Passover, for example) and work is permitted on this day. You may ask why we observe it if we don't have to. The answer is: Because we like this holiday. Lag B'Omer still retains the long-treasured memories of the heroic struggle our forefathers waged for the sake of the Torah. Because of that determined struggle we live today as Jews. As you read about Lag B'Omer you will discover that we associate this ancient holiday, which originated nearly 2,000 years ago, with the modern Yom Ha'Atzmaut, Israel's Independence Day. Why? You will find out as you read the WHY section, which gives the reason for observing this festival. The HOW part explains the manner of its observance.

The "Terms" and the "Numbers" should prove both helpful and enjoyable. Share them with your family and friends. Learning together makes for increased delight in this exciting day.

Finally, the material in "For Further Reading" contains books, pamphlets, reference works, etc., that will broaden your knowledge regarding this holiday. Read as many as you can.

A HAPPY LAG B'OMER TO YOU!

THE WHY OF LAG B'OMER

Until the birth of the State of Israel in 1948 Lag B'Omer had been the youngest of our Jewish festivals. Yet it was nearly 2,000 years ago that this "youngster" was born. It happened in the days when the Romans ruled Israel with an iron hand after defeating the Jews in two wars. They forbade the Jews to study the Torah and made life extremely bitter for them. Out of all this war and suffering came the festival of Lag B'Omer. Let us see what brought it into being.

After the Jews lived through many centuries of growth and progress punctuated by much suffering, beginning with the period of the Bible, followed by centuries of foreign rule, they were finally—after a short period of independence—conquered by the Romans, the mightiest rulers of ancient times. Then, when they rebelled against their Roman masters, they were defeated in the year 70 C.E. The Temple in Jerusalem was destroyed and many Jews were driven from their land into all parts of the Roman Empire and elsewhere. However, even outside their land, they did not stop studying the Torah.

Then about 60 years later (around 130 C.E.) the Jews asked the Emperor Hadrian to allow them to rebuild the Temple. Hadrian agreed at first, but then changing his mind, he consented only on condition that Jerusalem be rebuilt not as a Jewish, but as a heathen city, where only Roman idols, and not Almighty God, would be worshipped. So great was the Jews' disappointment and so fierce their anger that they decided to rebel against Rome and to try once more to regain their independence. But in this war too the little band of Jews was defeated and their hopes for rebuilding their Temple were crushed.

This second rebellion against Rome was led by a brave and legendary warrior. His name was Bar Kochba. Well known for his mighty strength he was chosen as a leader by one of the most famous scholars of all times, Rabbi Akiba. For a while it appeared that Bar Kochba's army would defeat the Romans, but the mighty armies of Rome were too much for the Jews. Now the Roman conquerors made life for the Jews more miserable than ever.

However, when the Romans discovered that the Jews refused to die after two defeats, and that it was the study of the Torah that kept them alive, they decided to forbid all study of Torah. In this way, thought the Romans, Judea would be destroyed forever.

But the Jews were not frightened. They still did not lose hope but instead, continued to study the Torah faithfully. Now, it happened during the days of Rabbi Akiba, and during the seven weeks, or 49 days, between Passover and Shavuot, that a frightful epidemic broke out among his students, killing thousands of them. That is why this period of 49 days is one of sadness. The rabbis forbade the celebration of any happy events, such as weddings and parties during these 7 weeks. However, a strange thing occurred: the raging epidemic suddenly stopped on the 33rd day. On this one day of the Omer (49 day) period no students died. For this reason all the festivities that had been forbidden during this period, were henceforth permitted on the 33rd day, which is called "Lag B'Omer".

The term "Lag B'Omer" comes, first, from "Lag" which in Hebrew stands for 33 because it is comprised of the letter "Lamed" which has the numerical value of 30 and "Gimmel," 3. It comes also from the "omer" period during Temple days, when a measure of grain, called an "omer," was brought into the Temple for 49 days, or seven weeks. This ceremony, known as S'firat Ha Omer (Counting of the Omer) began with the 2nd day of Passover and ended on the 50th day, which was the Festival of Shavuot. But this period of the days of Rabbi Akiba also came to be known as the "S'firah" period, a time of great sadness.

Lag B'Omer is also known as "Scholars' Day" because it reminds us of the end of the plague that killed off so many famous and beloved scholars. Some of the noted rabbis who lived during this period were Rabbi Akiba (who, although totally ignorant and uneducated until 40 years of age, later became one of the greatest scholars Israel has ever known), Rabbi Simeon bar Yohai (who lived in a cave for 13 years when studying Torah was forbidden), and many others.

Many scholars of this era became martyrs; they gave up their lives rather than their study of the Torah. Chief among them was Rabbi Akiba whom the Romans cruelly tortured to death.

On the other hand, Lag B'Omer is a happy holiday because we remember the heroism of these beloved scholars. They live on as unforgettable examples.

This, then, is the message of Lag B'Omer: we are filled with pride in our Torah, which communicated such faith and courage to the Jews that even the harshest Roman laws and other later prohibitions could not keep them from living by its teachings and studying it in the face of all dangers.

*Lag B'Omer at the grave of Rabbi Simeon bar Yohai,
by E. M. Lilien.*

HOW WE OBSERVE LAG B'OMER

Unlike most Jewish festivals, Lag B'Omer is not a religious holiday. In other words, there are not any special prayers to be said on this day. It is not mentioned in the Bible and yet certain customs are observed on this unique holiday.

Lag B'Omer falls during the period of 49 days when the omer is counted. In Temple days an "omer" (a measure of freshly-cut barley) was brought into the Temple daily during this period in order to determine the exact number of days between Passover and Shavuot. Even today, we still count the omer but in a different manner.

139

Beginning with the second day of Passover and during the full 49 days, every evening, shortly after dark, we recite a specific blessing and prayer. In this prayer we mention the number of weeks and days that have passed since we began counting. Thus, on the 17th day, for example, we say "Today is 17 days, which constitute two weeks and three days in the Counting of the Omer." Lag B'Omer is, as we have seen, the 33rd day in this counting. This constitutes 4 weeks and 5 days. This day falls on the 18th day of the month of Iyar.

Today, as in ancient times, weddings, parties and other festivities forbidden during the days of this *S'firah* (counting) period are permitted on Lag B'Omer. Such events naturally make this day a happy one.

In addition, Lag B'Omer is a day for picnics and outings where the children enjoy much fun and pleasure. At such festivities bow-and-arrow contests (as a reminder of Rabbi Simeon bar Yohai's students who used to display to watchful Roman eyes bows and arrows instead of books) are held along with other games and sports activities.

In Israel, Lag B'Omer is also a day for bonfire celebrations. The most famous of these is usually held at the village of Meron, near the northern city of Safed. Simeon bar Yohai is said to be buried there. Huge crowds of pious Hassidim from all over Israel gather near Meron for this gay celebration. (For a detailed description of this and other Lag B'Omer customs, see B. Edidin, pp. 160-163.)

It is said that while Rabbi Simeon bar Yohai was hiding in his cave he wrote a famous holy book called the ZOHAR. In this book are found numerous meanings of the Torah. On Lag B'Omer many of the Hassidim study portions of the Zohar during the special celebrations at Meron.

These customs indicate that although Lag B'Omer is a younger festival, with far fewer customs and observances than our older and more familiar festivals have, it is nevertheless a holiday we all love and enjoy; first, because it stresses the high value of the Torah in the lives of us Jews and, secondly, because of the heroic efforts of our forefathers to regain their freedom as a nation. All through the nearly two thousand years that it has been celebrated, it has filled Jewish hearts with life and hope, proving that the well-known saying "Israel and the Torah are one and inseparable," is indeed true.

NAMES AND TERMS FOR LAG B'OMER

AKIBA	The famous rabbi and scholar who urged Jews to rebel against Rome
BAR KOCHBA	The military leader of the second war against Rome
BOW AND ARROW	The symbol connected with Lag B'Omer
COUNTING OF THE OMER	English for *S'firat Ha Omer*
HADRIAN	The Roman Emperor who forbade studying the Torah
LAG	The Hebrew numerical value of 33
LAG B'OMER	33rd day of the counting of the omer
MERON	The town near which Rabbi Simeon bar Yohai is said to be buried
OMER	A measure of grain brought into the Temple between Passover and Shavuot as a way of counting the days between these two festivals
ORAL LAW	The rabbinic law which grew out of a study of the Bible, but which was handed down from teacher to student, from mouth to mouth—orally, and not in written form until later
SCHOLAR'S DAY	A name given to Lag B'Omer
S'FIRAT HA OMER	The counting of the omer for 49 days
SIMEON BAR YOHAI	A famous rabbi who lived in a cave for 13 years
TALMUD	The Oral Law which grew out of the study of the Torah
ZOHAR	A famous book containing many sacred meanings of the Torah

NUMBERS RELATING TO LAG B'OMER

2   Lag B'Omer took place during the *2nd* war with Rome

7   The *seven* weeks during which the omer is counted

13   Rabbi Simeon bar Yohai hid in a cave for *13* years

18   Lag B'Omer comes on the *18th* of Iyar

33   The words *Lag B'Omer* mean the *33rd* day of the counting of the omer

40   Rabbi Akiba was *forty* years old when he first began to study the Torah

49   The omer is counted for *49* days

SIGNIFICANT DATES TO REMEMBER ON LAG B'OMER

63 B.C.E.*

       70 C.E.**

            135 C.E.

---

  *B.C.E. stands for Before Common Era
**C.E. stands for Common Era

QUIZ QUESTIONS FOR LAG B'OMER

QUESTIONS:

1. Which nation ruled over Israel when Lag B'Omer took place?
2. Which Jewish practice is connected with Lag B'Omer?
3. a) How many times were the Jews defeated by the Romans?
   b) When?
4. Why did the Jews rebel against the Romans around the time of Lag B'Omer?
5. Give the approximate date of Lag B'Omer.
6. Who were the following?
   a) Bar Kochba
   b) Rabbi Akiba
7. Correct the following sentence: "Bar Kochba's armies were defeated throughout the entire war."
8. Why did the Romans forbid the study of the Torah?
9. a) What caused the 49-day period to become one of sadness?
   b) On which of these days are festivities permitted?
   c) Why?
10. Give the Hebrew date of Lag B'Omer.
11. How do we get the name "Lag B'Omer"?

ANSWERS:

1. Rome
2. Study of the Torah
3. a) Twice
   b) In 70 C.E. and about 130 C.E.
4. Because the Romans refused to let them rebuild the Temple as a Jewish house of worship
5. 135 C.E.
6. a) The military leader of the second war against Rome
   b) The famous scholar who chose Bar Kochba to lead the revolt
7. At first he won, but in the end he lost
8. They had discovered that studying the Torah had kept Judaism alive; prohibiting it, they thought, would destroy it
9. a) A plague killed off many famous scholars
   b) The 33rd day, Lag B'Omer
   c) The plague stopped that day
10. 18th day of Iyar
11. From the numerical value of the Hebrew letters "lamed" and "gimel"

12. When and for how long is the omer counted?

12. For 49 days, from Passover to Shavuot

13. Why is Lag B'Omer known as "Scholar's Day"?

13. Many great scholars died in the plague of that period

14. What is unusual about each of the following scholars?
    a) Rabbi Akiba
    b) Rabbi Simeon bar Yohai

14. a) He had been ignorant until he was 40 years of age
    b) He hid in a cave for 13 years

15. Why is Lag B'Omer a happy holiday?

15. a) The plague in which many scholars had died stopped on that day
    b) It gives us the hope that the Torah will always live no matter what harm our enemies may do us

16. What does Lag B'Omer have in common with holidays such as Tu Bishvat and Israel's Independence Day?

16. It is not a religious festival

17. What was an "omer"?

17. A measure of freshly-cut grain that was brought into the Temple during the weeks between Passover and Shavuot

18. a) How was the omer counted during the days of the Temple?

    b) Why was this done?

    c) How do we count it today?

18. a) An omer would be brought into the Temple every night between Passover and Shavuot

    b) To count the exact number of days between these two festivals

    c) Every night after dark we recite a special prayer in which we mention the number of days counted so far

19. a) Name a few ways in which Lag B'Omer is observed today.
    b) Why are bows and arrows used on Lag B'Omer?

19. a) Holding weddings, parties and other joyous events
    b) As a reminder of Rabbi Simeon bar Yohai's students who carried bows and arrows instead of books

20. a) Where, in Israel, is a famous bonfire celebration held?
    b) Why there?

21. What is the Zohar?

22. About how many years passed since Israel was last independent before the establishment of the present state?

23. What did the Roman persecution fail to do to the Jews?

24. For what two reasons should we always remember Lag B'Omer?

25. a) Which of the following does not belong here?
    Tu Bishvat, Lag B'Omer, Passover, Israel's Independence Day
    b) Why not?

20. a) At Meron, in northern Israel
    b) Rabbi Simeon bar Yohai is said to be buried there

21. A holy book about the Torah which Simeon bar Yohai is said to have written while in the cave

22. About 2,000 years

23. Stop them from studying the Torah

24. a) The great value of the Torah for our lives as Jews
    b) The heroic struggle of our forefathers to regain their national freedom

25. a) Passover
    b) It is a major festival while the others are minor holidays

SUMMARY AND COMPARISON OF LAG B'OMER AND ISRAEL'S INDEPENDENCE DAY

Even though Lag B'Omer and Israel's Independence Day appear to be two distinct and separate festivals, there is a close link that joins them. That is, it is not merely a coincidence that both festivals come so close together during the same month. But both are also closely related to one another in other ways.

The struggle for Jewish survival against the Romans that began with Lag B'Omer was finally won nearly 2,000 years later with the birth of the State of Israel. Following the Jews' defeat in their second war with Rome, they had nothing but their Torah to keep them alive as Jews. But, it was the nourishment of the Torah and its study which enabled them to stay alive until the turn of events of the 20th century also won them national independence. In other words, without the Torah, Jewish survival until 1948 would have been impossible.

Going back to the days of Rabbi Akiba, just suppose that one of his students, carrying a bow and arrow, would have shot at a target, which we will call "national independence." Of course, he, no doubt missed that target at that time, because Roman might was far too strong for Israel. But, let us continue to imagine as though that same arrow (or, another one shot immediately afterward) had sailed on and on for 2,000 years, all the way up to the year 1948. At that time it finally did hit its mark, namely, the freedom won by the present independent State of Israel.

This long struggle for national freedom is but another shining example of the hope and optimism which fills the heart of every loyal Jew. But this feeling of hope did not come from nowhere. It was founded on the firm foundation of the soundness of that same Torah which has kept the Jew alive throughout the ages. Never has that hope been lost, not even during Judaism's darkest days.

Furthermore, the Jew always felt that only in his own land, in Israel, could he ever live a full and complete life as a Jew.

It is, therefore, now up to us to see that that independence remains, because the freedom we have won is to be of use, not for ourselves alone but also for the well-being of all of mankind. Israel's miraculous progress during the past 30 years, when so many other nations have benefited from her advances in science, literature, education, and other such fields, is but a small sample of what a free and independent Israel can do. This is what Israel has been doing with its freedom ever since it won it. Isn't it worth protecting with all that we have, with our energies, our money, our support and love and with everything else of value?

Let us think about such questions as we celebrate Israel's birthday with pride and joy in our hearts.

SHAVUOT

Bringing of the first harvest.
(Courtesy Israel Information Services.)

Shavuot is a very unusual festival. The shortest of all the major holidays, it lasts but two days (in Israel, only one day). But "Good things come in small packages." Shavuot certainly does. The WHY of this chapter explains its meaning and value. As you will see, Shavuot is a strong link in the unbroken chain of our festivals. How is this possible? Read the WHY and find out!

However, all the reasons have meaning only if they are put into practice. The HOW shows what to do for Shavuot and how to enjoy it. Some of these practices apply to other festivals as well, but many of them are reserved for Shavuot alone.

Since Shavuot is closely associated with the Ten Commandments, these are included here. Study them, try to learn more about them. The section "For Further Reading" suggests some sources of additional information for these and other relevant topics.

The more you learn about this lovely festival, the more you will enjoy it.

HAPPY YOM TOV!

WHY WE OBSERVE SHAVUOT

Like Passover and Sukkot, Shavuot is one of the Three Pilgrimage Festivals ("Shalosh Regalim"), each of which is observed for both a historical and agricultural reason. However, of all the festivals, Shavuot is the shortest, lasting but two days (one day in Israel). But this does not signify that it is less important than the others. On the contrary, Shavuot is best-known for one of the most outstanding events in the entire history of the Jewish people—the receiving of the Ten Commandments on Mount Sinai. Because of this highly significant event, this is usually designated as the "Torah Festival," or more accurately as *Z'man Mattan Toratenu* (the Season of the Giving of Our Law). There is no doubt that the receiving of the Torah changed the course of Jewish history and gave the Jew his most valid reason for living as a Jew. In fact, the outstanding Jewish scholar, Saadia Gaon, has said that we are a people only because of our Torah. This fact alone would be sufficient reason to make Shavuot one of the mightiest pillars supporting Judaism's structure. It was the Torah that gave life and substance to the Jew no matter where he lived and what he did, whether in his homeland Israel, or anywhere else in the world. Thus, his Torah became a *Torat Chayim*, a Tree of Life.

The story of how the Torah was given to the Israelites through Moses on Mount Sinai is quite a familiar one. A full account of it may be found in the Bible (Exodus, chapters 19-20). But, around this tale countless legends have been woven, telling us more about the circumstances of this memorable event. (See Goldin's *Jewish Legends*, Vol. I, pp. 355, ff.) One of these is the oft-told tale how all the nations of the world refused to accept the Torah, but only Israel received it gladly and without question.

We must also remember that the Torah which Israel received on Mount Sinai included in full, in addition to the Ten Commandments, both the Written Law and the Oral Law, which grew out of the former. The term Torah applies therefore to both the Written and the Oral Law.

In fact, it is said that the Jews became a free people because they accepted the Torah. Thus, the physical freedom won by the exodus from Egypt led to the spiritual freedom at Mount Sinai because even though the Israelites were no longer slaves after they had left Egypt, they were still enslaved to many idolatrous ideas until they accepted the Torah. In this way does Passover lead up to Shavuot.

Shavuot and Passover are related in yet another way. Since Passover marked the beginning of the grain season in Israel, the Israelites were commanded to bring into the Temple for a period of 49 days or seven weeks, starting with the second day of the Festival, a measure called an *omer* of freshly-cut barley. The 50th day was Shavuot. That is why Shavuot is called the "Feast of Weeks." (The "Counting of the Omer" is still observed today, but now it is done by reciting a blessing and a prayer during every one of the 49 days.) In English, Shavuot is also called "Pentecost," a term derived from the Greek and meaning a festival of the 50th day.

Because the early crops (especially the barley) ripened around the time of Shavuot, this festival is known in the Bible as *Chag Ha Bikkurim*, the Festival of First Fruits. This aspect of the festival assumed the form of thanksgiving which led to a number of beautiful ceremonies. Some of these will be described in the HOW section. In the Bible, although it is perhaps best-known as *Chag Ha Bikkurim*, Shavuot is referred to by another name, too: *Chag Ha Katzir*, that is, The Festival of the Harvest, when the early crops were harvested.

In addition to the historical and agricultural reasons so far given for the observance of Shavuot, there is still another, a lesser one. This festival recalls to our minds the anniversary of the death of King David, who was a descendant of Ruth, as mentioned in the Book of Ruth (see the HOW section).

We are taught that from the family of King David will come forth the Messiah, who will usher in a period of peace, freedom and security for all the people of Israel, on its native soil in the Land of Israel. This becomes another message for the Festival of Shavuot.

From the foregoing it can be seen that the two basic reasons for observing Shavuot—the historical and the agricultural—blend into one harmonious whole. This means that both the historical aspect of Shavuot (which makes it the Torah Festival) and its agricultural aspect (the Bikkurim and early harvest) may be considered the serious and the happy ways of looking at this holiday.

But despite its solemn side, Shavuot is on the whole a happy festival, meant to lead to happiness. For example, the giving of the Torah was intended to add to our joy, because the Israelites felt grateful for this precious gift of Torah.

However, the meaning and purpose of Shavuot can be most clearly understood from its observances. Let us see what forms of observance it has to offer as we read the following section, the HOW of Shavuot.

HOW SHAVUOT IS OBSERVED

Even though the Festival of Shavuot lasts but two days, it nevertheless entails a number of observances. Here are the most important of them.

As Shavuot celebrates the receiving of our Torah, it is only natural that we read the story of the Ten Commandments on that day. Therefore, in the synagogue the Torah reading for the first day covers the portion that describes this unique event, found in Exodus 19-20. Everyone stands while the Ten Commandments are being read.

But, as has already been said, more than the Ten Commandments were given on Mount Sinai on the 6th day of Sivan. All 613 precepts of the Torah were given then too. In addition, also the Oral Law (which explains and clarifies all of these) was likewise included.

For this reason, on the first night of Shavuot a special booklet called a *Tikkun* is read and studied. This *Tikkun* contains portions from all 39 Books of the Bible, as well as from certain other sacred writings. In this way it becomes possible to review the essence of the entire Torah in a single night. Many pious Jews sit up throughout the night studying this *Tikkun* and other such works. This is but another example of the Jew's deep love for the Torah.

Since the Torah tells of the *Shloshet Y'may Hagbalah* (The Three Days of Preparation) during which time the Israelites were commanded to prepare themselves for this momentous event, we also remember these days as a period of preparation for the coming of Shavuot. During these days certain prayers of a sorrowful nature are omitted, nor do any of the restrictions of the *S'firah* (Counting) period apply.

During the synagogue services of the first day, just as the Torah is about to be read, a beautiful prayer in a form of a poem is recited. This prayer, written in Aramaic, and called *Akdamot*, is chanted. It tells of God's love for Israel, of devotion to the Torah, and of the hope for the Messiah. As on all other festivals, special prayers and Torah readings are provided for Shavuot. Also, on the second day the *Yizkor* (Memorial Service) is recited in memory of the departed.

The special *Megilla* (Scroll) read on Shavuot is the Book of Ruth. This short book (found in the Holy Writings) tells of Ruth, a young Moabite woman, who chose to convert to Judaism. One of her later descendants was King David. It also pictures some of the agricultural life of the ancient Hebrews, especially during the harvest season. This brings us to the agricultural aspect of Shavuot.

The first sheep shearing festival at a settlement in the Hills of Judea. (Courtesy Keren Hayesod.)

During the days of the Temple this festival was observed as a happy harvest celebration for the grain and other early-ripened crops. From the second day of Passover until Shavuot the exact number of days was counted by bringing into the Temple a measure (called an *omer*) of fresh-cut barley, for a period of 49 days or seven weeks. The 50th day was then celebrated as **Chag Ha Shavuot**, or the *Feast of Weeks*, thus giving the festival its name.

Also during this period, each Israelite farmer would set aside the first of his crops as they ripened and bring them to the Temple by Shavuot, the time for the second annual pilgrimage to Jerusalem. The *Bikkurim* (first fruits) provided a most colorful scene as they were brought ceremoniously to the Temple. The ceremony of presenting them to the *Kohen* (priest) in the Temple (in a special basket called a *Teneh*) is described in the Bible (Deuteronomy 26:1-11). This was another form of expressing thanks to God for His kindness to man.

But today, since most Jews live outside the Land of Israel, hardly any of these agricultural customs have survived. One possible remnant of Temple days is the custom of eating dairy foods on Shavuot. This serves as a reminder of the farm life of our ancestors, but many other explanations have been suggested for this custom. The special delicacy eaten on Shavuot is *blintzes*.

Another Shavuot custom reminiscent of ancient times is that of decorating the synagogue and the home with flowers and leaves. These may perhaps be another reminder of Mount Sinai which was green with plants and shrubs. Also, it may be a symbol of the harvest which was brought to the Temple.

In addition to the customs so far mentioned there are also a few less important ones which originated at a later date. For centuries custom ordained that Shavuot be the first day on which a small child was to begin his Hebrew education. After being brought to the synagogue he would be taken to the school for a special ceremony which marked the formal start of his Jewish education.

In the past hundred years or so, it has been customary to hold Confirmation Exercises on Shavuot, especially in Reform and Conservative congregations. This may be a substitute for the above-mentioned custom of beginning a child's Hebrew education on Shavuot. These exercises, denoting the completion of a period of studies, are thus connected with the study of the Torah.

In our own days the Bikkurim ceremony has been revived in Israel. Even though the *Bikkurim* could be offered only in Jerusalem while the Temple was still standing, it is celebrated today in a more colorful festivity, not only in Jerusalem, but also in many other parts of the country. (For a detailed description, see B. Edidin's *Jewish Holidays And Festivals* pp. 174-176.)

Shavuot is the only holiday to which you keep looking forward by counting the days until it arrives. This we do when we count the Omer from Passover on. Then, when it finally does arrive, what do we have? Only a two-day festival! But see the delightful ways we have of observing it—eating blintzes, decorating with greens, reading about Ruth, to mention only a few.

However, each and every one of these customs can enrich our lives as we keep our glorious past alive, and at the same time, light the way into the future. Therefore, make the most of Shavuot. You have only two days to do so.

A HAPPY YOM TOV!

THE TEN COMMANDMENTS

I
I AM THE LORD THY GOD WHO BROUGHT THEE OUT OF THE LAND OF EGYPT

II
THOU SHALT HAVE NO OTHER GODS BEFORE ME

III
THOU SHALT NOT TAKE THE LORD'S NAME IN VAIN

IV
REMEMBER THE SABBATH DAY AND KEEP IT HOLY

V
HONOR THY FATHER AND THY MOTHER

VI
THOU SHALT NOT KILL

VII
THOU SHALT NOT COMMIT ADULTERY

VIII
THOU SHALT NOT STEAL

IX
THOU SHALT NOT BEAR FALSE WITNESS AGAINST THY NEIGHBOR

X
THOU SHALT NOT COVET

TERMS FOR SHAVUOT

AKDAMOT	A special poem read on Shavuot
BIKKURIM	First Fruits, which were brought to the Temple as an offering on Shavuot
BLINTZES	The favorite food for Shavuot
BOAZ	Ruth's second husband
BOOK OF RUTH	The Megilla read on Shavuot
CHAG HA BIKKURIM	"Festival of First Fruits," a name for Shavuot
CHAG HA KATZIR	"Festival of the Harvest," a name for Shavuot
CHAG HA SHAVUOT	"Feast of Weeks"
FEAST OF WEEKS	A name for Shavuot
FESTIVAL OF FIRST FRUITS	A name for Shavuot
FESTIVAL OF THE HARVEST	A name for Shavuot
HONOR THY FATHER AND THY MOTHER	The fifth of the Ten Commandments
KING DAVID	The great-grandson of Ruth and Boaz, and one of the most famous kings of Israel
KOHEN	The priest in the Temple to whom the Bikkurim offerings were given on Shavuot
LEKET	The tiny bits of harvested grain which were to be left behind for the poor during the harvest season
MESSIAH	The descendant of King David who will come and enable the Jews to return to their homeland Israel
MOUNT SINAI	The place where the Ten Commandments were given
NAOMI	Ruth's mother-in-law who brought her from Moab to Judah
OMER	The measure of grain which was to be brought into the Temple during seven weeks from Passover to Shavuot

ORAL LAW	That body of laws which explains the Torah, the Written Law
PEAH	The grain which could be harvested by the poor from four corners of every field during the harvest session
PENTECOST	Another name for Shavuot
RUTH	The Moabite woman, Naomi's daughter-in-law, who accepted the Jewish religion; the great-grandmother of King David
SEASON OF THE GIVING OF THE LAW	A name for Shavuot
S'FIRAH	The seven-week period when the omer is counted
SHICH'CHAH	The grain that was forgotten in the fields (or elsewhere) and was to be left behind for the poor
SHLOSHET Y'MAY HAGBALAH	The Three Days of Preparation
SHALOSH REGALIM	The Three Festivals of Rejoicing
SIVAN	The Hebrew month in which Shavuot comes
TENEH	The special basket in which the Bikkurim offerings were presented to the Kohen on Shavuot
THREE DAYS OF PREPARATION	The three days before the Ten Commandments were to be given during which time the Israelites were to prepare themselves for the great event
THREE FESTIVALS OF REJOICING	The three festivals: PESAH, SHAVUOT, AND SUKKOT, when pilgrimages were made to Jerusalem
TIKKUN	The special booklet, read the first night of Shavuot, which contains small portions of every Book of the Bible and other holy writings
WRITTEN LAW	The Torah, which contains the basic laws of Judaism
Z'MAN MATTAN TORATENU	The Season of the Giving of Our Law, a name for Shavuot

NUMBERS FOR SHAVUOT

2	Shavuot lasts *two* days
	The *Two* Tablets of the Law
	We begin counting the Omer on the *2nd* day of Passover
3	The *three* days of preparation
	Sivan is the *3rd* month of the year
5	The *Five* Books of Moses
6	The first day of Shavuot is on the *6th* of Sivan
7	The second day of Shavuot is on the *7th* day of Sivan
	The *seven* weeks of the counting of the Omer
10	The *Ten* Commandments
39	There are *39* Books in the whole Bible
49	The seven weeks of the Omer counting consist of *49* days
50	Shavuot is the *50th* day after the seven weeks of counting
248	In the Torah *248* of the Commandments say "You *shall* Do!"
365	There are *365* Commandments which say, "You shall *Not* Do!"
613	The laws in the Torah amount to *613* in all

QUIZ QUESTIONS FOR SHAVUOT

QUESTIONS:

1. What does the term Chag Ha Shavuot mean?
2. To which group of festivals does Shavuot belong?
3. Give 2 other names for Shavuot.
4. How many days does Shavuot last?
5. What is the Hebrew date of Shavuot?
6. Why is Shavuot called "Feast of Weeks"?
7. a) Is Shavuot a major or a minor Festival?
   b) How can you tell?
8. For what reason in Jewish history do we observe Shavuot?
9. What were the "Shloshet Y'may Hagbalah"?
10. Where were the Ten Commandments given?
11. How long after the Israelites had left Egypt was the Torah given to them?
12. Were the Israelites the first and only people to be offered the Torah?

ANSWERS:

1. Feast of Weeks
2. The Three Festivals of Rejoicing
3. *Z'man Mattan Toratenu* (Season of the Giving of Our Law) *Chag Ha Bikkurim* (Festival of Early Fruits)
4. Two
5. 6th and 7th of Sivan
6. Because of the seven weeks which are counted between Passover and Shavuot
7. a) Major
   b) It is mentioned in the Torah as one of the Holy Days when work is forbidden
8. The Giving of the Ten Commandments
9. The Three Days of Preparation, which came three days before the Torah was given
10. On Mount Sinai
11. Seven Weeks
12. No. It was offered to other peoples also, but they all refused to accept it for one reason or another

13. Give the fifth of the Ten Commandments.

14. How many of the Ten Commandments can you name?

15. What is an important difference between the first five and the last five of the Ten Commandments?

16. a) Into how many major parts is the whole Bible divided?
    b) Name them.

17. a) How many laws are there in the whole Torah?
    b) Of these, how many are "do's" and how many are "don'ts"?

13. Honor Thy Father and Thy Mother

14. (Look them up, if you have to)

15. The first five are commandments which pertain to behavior between man and God, and the second five—between man and man

16. a) Three
    b) *Torah* (Law), *Prophets* and *Holy Writings*

17. a) 613
    b) "Do's"-248; "Don'ts"-365

Arbor Day on the outskirts of Tel Aviv.
(Courtesy Keren Hayesod.)

18. Which book of the Five Scrolls is read on Shavuot?
18. The Book of Ruth

19. From which land did Ruth come?
19. Moab

20. What was the relationship between Naomi and Ruth?
20. Naomi was Ruth's mother-in-law

21. Who was Boaz?
21. The second husband of Ruth

22. What famous king of Israel was descended from Ruth and Boaz?
22. King David

23. Name the agricultural reason for observing Shavuot.
23. It reminds us of the grain harvest in ancient Israel

24. What is meant by the *Bikkurim* observance?
24. The offerings which the Israelites used to bring to the Temple on Shavuot

25. What is the meaning of the word *Bikkurim?*
25. The Hebrew word for Early Fruits, or the first to ripen

26. What was the important crop which was harvested in ancient Israel before the Shavuot Festival?
26. Wheat, also barley

27. Give the meaning of the Hebrew word *Teneh.*
27. The special basket in which the Bikkurim offerings were placed before the priest

28. On which day of Shavuot are the Ten Commandments read?
28. The first

29. What must everyone in the synagogue do when the Ten Commandments are read?
29. Stand

30. Name the special book of sacred writings which is read on the first night of Shavuot.
30. The *Tikkun*

31. What is a Tikkun?
31. A special book read on the first night of Shavuot which contains portions taken from the Bible, Talmud and other holy books

32. a) What is meant by *Akdamot?*
    b) On which day is it read?
32. a) Name of a special poem read during the Shavuot services
    b) The first day

159

33. How are the home and synagogue decorated on Shavuot?

33. With green leaves and branches

34. What types of food are eaten on Shavuot?

34. Dairy foods

35. Name a special food eaten on Shavuot.

35. Blintzes

36. a) What is meant by "Oral Law"?
    b) In what books is it found?
    c) How is it related to Shavuot?

36. a) Those laws which explain the "Written Law," Torah
    b) The Talmud
    c) Both the Written and the Oral Law were given on Mount Sinai

37. Why was Shavuot an important day in the life of a small child many years ago?

37. On that day he started school

38. In ancient times, what were three ways the poor could get grain during the harvest season?

38. a) *Shich'chah*—grain that was forgotten by its owner
    b) *Leket*—gleanings, that is, the small bits of harvested grain
    c) *Peah*—the four corners of the field which were left unharvested

39. a) Which famous Jewish king's passing is remembered on Shavuot?
    b) Why?

39. a) King David
    b) He was descended from Ruth and Boaz

40. What meaning do the following numbers have in connection with Shavuot?
    2, 3, 10, 50, and 613

40. 2—*Two* days of Shavuot and the *Two* Tablets of the Law
    3—*Three* days of preparation
    10—*Ten* Commandments
    50—Shavuot is the *50th* day beginning with 2nd day of Passover, when the counting of the Omer begins
    613—The whole Torah contains *613* Commandments

FAST-DAYS

Out of the depths.

Jeremiah, by E. M. Lilien.

No doubt you already know that we Jews fast at certain times of the year. But have you ever known or understood when or why we fast? Or what fasting does for us? This chapter explains these as well as other questions.

Perhaps you think fasting is only sad or unpleasant. In that case you have a surprise in store for you on the following pages.

What is more, since there are several fasts scattered through the Jewish year, a special table summarizing all these fast-days has been prepared for you. Study it as you go along as well as when you finish the WHY and HOW sections.

The "Terms" and "Numbers" will also help you understand the reading material better. Then, as in all previous HOW and WHY portions, these features may be used to provide fun and enjoyment in the form of games, contests, etc. Some of these features may be real eye-openers for you.

Finally, reading the books listed under "For Further Reading" will broaden your knowledge of Jewish life and give you a fuller and clearer understanding of what this chapter has told you.

The total result will be that you will know why we Jews fast and how fasting has contributed to make us an eternal people. No wonder one of the popular sayings among Jews is: "AM YISROEL HAI!" (THE JEWISH PEOPLE LIVES!).

By keeping yourself properly informed about Judaism, you will be helping it to live forever.

WHY WE OBSERVE OUR JEWISH FAST-DAYS

We come now to some special days that are quite different from most of the festivals studied so far. These days are called the Jewish "Fast-Days." Of course, the word "fasting" immediately makes you think of Yom Kippur. True, we do fast on Yom Kippur, but we also fast on certain other days. All of these special days will be described here.

Most of these fast-days (when we are forbidden to *eat* or *drink* anything at all)* are also days of sadness. You may ask: But why do we have to be sad? Can't we be happy all the time? In answer to these questions, suppose you look at a colored picture. When you see the dark and shadowy colors, don't the bright colors appear to be much brighter than they would be if there were no dark colors for contrast in between? Color-wise, that is just how our Jewish holidays would look if they were all painted in different colors; some would be brighter and others darker.

However, not all our fast-days are necessarily days of sadness. Thus, Yom Kippur, the Day of Atonement, the most important of all fast-days, is not a day of mourning or gloom but a day expressing hope, trust and joy.**

THE NATURE OF THE JEWISH FASTS

Every Jewish fast is either a major or a minor one. A major fast lasts from one evening until the next evening, a full twenty-four hours. Of these fasts there are only two, Yom Kippur and Tisha B'Av (the ninth of Av).

A minor fast begins at sunrise and ends at sunset of the same day. Also, for major fasts there are more restrictions and prohibitions than for the minor fasts. Thus, on both Yom Kippur and Tisha B'Av washing yourself and wearing leather shoes are forbidden.

---

* Even if you are under thirteen years of age (the required age for fasting), you can still do your part by trying to fast. See *Yom Kippur* chapter.
** For an example of the joy felt on Yom Kippur, see B. Edidin, p. 68. Also see our chapter on Yom Kippur.

WHICH ARE THE JEWISH FASTS?*

We Jews observe a total of seven regular fast-days a year, as follows:

1) Major Fasts—*Yom Kippur* and *Tisha B'Av*

2) Minor Fasts—10th of Tevet, 17th of Tammuz, Fast of Gedaliah, Fast of Esther, Fast of the First-born (*Ta'anit B'chorim*).

In addition to these officially-commanded fasts, there are also a number of private, or personal, fasts. Thus, for example, it is customary for a bride and groom to fast on their wedding day. And some people even fast on the anniversary of a dear one's death.**

Also, special fasts are sometimes decreed by rabbinical authorities in times of national emergency and crisis. For example, in June 1967 while the Six-Day war was being fought in Israel, a half-day of fasting was decreed to pray for the Israeli armies' victory.

TISHA B'AV (THE NINTH OF AV)

This fast is the saddest day of the Jewish year. That is because both the First Temple (which King Solomon had built) and the Second Temple (which the returning exiles from Babylonia had rebuilt) were destroyed on this same date, but hundreds of years apart. The First Temple fell to the Babylonians in the year 586 B.C.E. and the Second Temple in 70 C.E., following Judea's defeat in its war against Rome.

After the destruction of each of these two Temples, the Jews were driven from their land into Exile (*Galut*), in 586 B.C.E. to Babylonia, and in 70 C.E. into the Great Exile throughout the world there to wander for 2,000 years. This punishment in itself would have been sufficient reason to make us mourn on Tisha B'Av.

But, as though such a terrible blow were not enough for our people, a number of additional sad events occurred also on the 9th of Av. Here are but a few of them.

---

* For this chapter consult table "Summary of the Jewish Fasts."
** For other examples of private fasts, see Y. Vainstein's *The Cycle of the Jewish Year*, pp. 168-9.

1. The Israelites, following their Exodus from Egypt, on the 9th of Av were told that they would have to wander in the desert for 40 years.

2. Betar, a powerful Jewish stronghold, fell to the Romans in 135 C.E. on the 9th of Av.

3. The Jews of Spain were expelled from that land on the 9th of Av in 1492 (just a few months before Columbus set sail for the New World).

4. The beginning of World War I, in 1914, was on this day.

Little wonder, then, that our rabbis called this day "A day set for misfortunes," or "The Black Fast."

All this notwithstanding, Tisha B'Av is not all sadness; it is also a day of hope and promise. Our Sages say that the Messiah (who will come, in his time, to redeem the Jews of the world) was born on this day. It was their hope (as well as ours today) that the day would come when Tisha B'Av, along with all other fast-days, would be turned into a day of joy and gladness.

The manner in which Tisha B'Av, as well as the minor fasts, should be observed is explained in the HOW section.

THE MINOR FASTS

The Tenth of Tevet

This fast aims to remind us of the days of the First Temple when, in 588 B.C.E., the Babylonian armies first began to surround the walls of Jerusalem. This step marked the beginning of the end of the Kingdom of Judah and later led to its final destruction, as well as the burning of the Temple two years later, in 586 B.C.E.

The 17th of Tammuz

It was on this day in 586 B.C.E. that the mighty armies of Babylonia under their king, Nebuchadnezzar, made the first breach in the walls surrounding Jerusalem. Three weeks later, on the ninth of Av, they captured the city and destroyed the Temple. This tragedy was another reason for sadness and fasting.

Other events that are said to have taken place on the 17th of Tammuz are:

1. Moses broke the first set of the Tablets of the Ten Commandments.
2. The daily sacrifices in the Temple (especially during the second one) had to stop on this day.
3. Apostomus, a Syrian general (in the time of the Second Temple), set up an idol in the Temple.

Fast of Gedaliah (Tzom Gedaliah)

This fast, which comes on the 3rd of Tishri, the day after Rosh HaShana, recalls the grief the Jews suffered following the murder of Gedaliah, whom the Babylonians had appointed governor of Judah after its defeat in 586 B.C.E. The Jews felt crushed by his death. They had placed great hopes upon him and now believed that his downfall meant yet another defeat for their nation. Hence this day has become one of mourning and fasting.

Fast of Esther (on the day before Purim)

Before Queen Esther (of the Purim story) went before King Ahasuerus to beg him to save her fellow-Jews from the wicked Haman, she promised her cousin Mordecai that she and her maidens would fast three days and three nights. She told Mordecai to order all the Jews of Persia to fast and pray with her.

This fast comes on the day before Purim. But whenever Purim falls on a Sunday, this fast is held on the preceding Thursday, since fasting is forbidden on a Friday or a Sabbath (except for Yom Kippur).

Fast of the First-Born (Ta'anit B'chorim)

This is a "fast" (on the day before Passover) that is not even observed as a fast. The following is the reason: Every first born Jewish child ought to fast on this day as a way of thanking God for having saved the Israelites' first-born when the Angel of Death was killing all the first-born children of the Egyptians, just before the Israelites' exodus from Egypt. However, if these *B'chorim* (first-born) study and complete a portion of the Talmud, they are exempt from fasting, for they are then considered to have paid proper respect to the Israelites' first-born.

WHY DO WE FAST?

You may still be wondering: Why do we have to fast? What does fasting do for us? There are several reasons for fasting; the following are a few of them:

1. *Forgiveness of sins*:

The best example of a fast-day is, of course, Yom Kippur. As we stand before the Almighty begging Him for life during the coming year, we show Him that we are sincere by fasting. Eating would be a sign of contentment and disinterest in God's judgment.

2. *Reminder of national tragedies*:

Each of the minor fasts such as the Tenth of Tevet, the 17th of Tammuz, and the Fast of Gedaliah, as well as the Ninth of Av, is a sort of a "Memorial Day." On each of these special days we pause to recall a great loss which our people suffered on that date.

3. *Prayer for God's help in a crisis*:

This was the reason for the Fast of Esther, when she risked her life by going before the king to beg for the lives of her people, as for the half-day fast during the Six-Day War in Israel in 1967 (as mentioned above).

In addition to these three basic reasons there are also special occasions when private fasts are observed. (See p. 164 above.)

The HOW section that follows describes what we do on these various fast-days.

HOW THE JEWISH FASTS ARE OBSERVED

The following summary of observances on fast-days indicates the chief difference between the major and the minor fasts. Study them carefully and compare them.

Major Fasts (*Yom Kippur and the Fast of Av*)

Last from one evening to the following evening;
Have more restrictions and prohibitions than the minor fasts;
Most work is forbidden;
No leather footwear may be worn;
If it falls on a Sabbath, then:

> Yom Kippur is observed with but a few changes
> Fast of Av is postponed until the following day (as are minor fasts).

Minor Fasts (all except the two mentioned above)

Last from sunrise to sunset of the same day;
Have fewer restrictions than major fasts;
Regular work is permitted;
If it falls on a Sabbath, it is either:

>Postponed to the following day, or,
>Observed a few days earlier (as is the Fast of Esther).

On All Fast-Days

Most of the regular prayers are recited.
Special prayers are recited, as well as special Torah and Haftorah readings.
No joyous events are permitted.

The saddest of all the fast-days are those within the three weeks extending from the Seventeenth of Tammuz through the Ninth of Av, inasmuch as it was during this period that the Temple was destroyed. Let us list some of the restrictions that apply to these mournful days.

From the 17th of Tammuz until the first of Av the following festivities and pleasures are forbidden: weddings or other joyous celebrations; playing music; cutting one's hair; wearing new clothes for the first time. However, a *B'rit Millah* (circumcision) celebration is permitted.

A special haftorah from the Book of Isaiah or Jeremiah is read on each Sabbath of these three weeks. In each haftorah the prophet rebukes the people for their sins and warns them of the punishment to come. The Sabbath before the Ninth of Av is called *Shabbat Hazon* because the latter word is the first in the haftorah from the Book of Isaiah.

Then, from the 1st of Av through the 9th, no meat may be eaten and no wine drunk, except on the Sabbath. Bathing and swimming are also forbidden.

On the eve of the Fast of Av a light meal is eaten just before the fast begins.

As we enter the synagogue on the eve of Tisha B'Av, we see the following changes inside: The lights are dim, and the worshippers sit either on the floor or on low stools, wearing no shoes at all or else footwear made without any leather (such as tennis shoes or sandals of rubber or straw). These last customs stand for mourning and grief. However, the closing portions of the Lamentations read night and morning contain expressions of comfort and hope that Zion (Israel) will some day be rebuilt.

On Tisha B'Av Day no work is permitted until the afternoon. The Sabbath following Tisha B'Av is called *Shabbat Nahamu* (The Sabbath of Comforting), so named after the opening word of the haftorah of that day. This Shabbat and the six that follow (until Rosh HaShana) are known as the "Seven Sabbaths of Comforting." On each of these Sabbaths the haftorah is from the Book of Isaiah, where the prophet speaks words of comfort and cheer to the Jews of his day.

On fast-days other than those within these three weeks, the restrictions are much less severe.

Now that we have learned what we must do for fasting, we may ask ourselves, *what does fasting do for us?*

1. First of all, as we feel those sharp pangs of hunger, we are reminded of the reason for fasting. Thus, on Yom Kippur, we can't help but remember that it is the Day of Atonement, when we ask forgiveness for our sins. Also, in order to show God that we are sincere, we punish our bodies by fasting. This latter thought applies to all the other fasts as well.

2. When we fast on days other than Yom Kippur, we are reminded of our past history and of how our people struggled to survive as a nation.

3. As we think over our history we feel closer to our people and we identify with them. Thus being part and parcel of them, we owe our people our full loyalty and devotion.

4. This certainly helps us gain hope and courage for the future. For while we fast and remember our people's heaviest blows, we also realize that our people survived and outlived all those who tried to destroy us, the Babylonians, Egyptians, Romans and many others. As we finish our fast we do so with renewed hope and determination to withstand all our future enemies.

This determination and "inner strength" comes primarily from the study of our Torah and the civilization that has been built on its teachings. These thoughts make us want to strive to reach that glorious day when we will no longer have to fast, when our present fast-days (except Yom Kippur) will be abolished and replaced by days of joy and gladness. Let us hope, pray and work for that blessed day!

SUMMARY OF THE JEWISH FAST-DAYS

Name of Fast	Date	Minor or Major	Reason	Extent of Sadness
Fast of Tevet	10th of Tevet	Minor	Siege of Jerusalem begun	Some
Fast of Tammuz	17th of Tammuz	Minor	First breach in wall of Jerusalem	Some
Fast of Av	9th of Av	Major	Both Temples destroyed	Much
Fast of Esther	13th of Adar	Minor	Esther's pleading for the lives of the Jews	Some
Fast of Gedaliah	3rd of Tishri	Minor	Murder of Gedaliah	Some
Fast of Yom Kippur	10th of Tishri	Major	Ask forgiveness for our sins	Little
Fast of First-Born	10th of Nissan	Minor	Give thanks for saving our first-born	None

TERMS FOR THE FAST-DAYS

APOSTOMUS	A Syrian general who set up an idol in the Temple on the 17th of Tammuz (during the days of the Second Temple)
AV	The fifth month of the Hebrew year, when the Fast of Av comes
B.C.E.	Before Common Era (used instead of "B.C.")
B'CHOR	First-born child in a family
BETAR	A powerful Hebrew stronghold which fell to the Romans on the Ninth of Av during Judea's second war with Rome
BLACK FAST	A special name given to Tisha B'Av because of the many misfortunes which occurred to the Jews on that day
BOOK OF LAMENTATIONS	One of the "Five Scrolls" of the Bible, read on the night of Tisha B'Av, describing the deep sorrow of the prophet Jeremiah when he witnessed the destruction of the First Temple
B'RIT MILLAH	The ceremony of circumcision for a male child on the eighth day of his birth
C.E.	Common Era (used instead of "A.D.")
ESTHER	Queen of Persia, mentioned in the Purim story, who fasted for three days before going to the king to save her people
FAST OF AV	English name for Tisha B'Av
FAST OF ESTHER	Fast that falls on the day before Purim, commemorating Queen Esther's efforts to save her people from Haman
FAST OF THE FIRST-BORN	Fast that falls on the day before Passover, commemorating thanks to God for having saved the Israelites' first-born children just before the exodus from Egypt
FAST OF GEDALIAH	Falls on the day after Rosh HaShana, in memory of the murder of Gedaliah, governor of the Jews

FASTING	The act of not eating or drinking for one full day or less, as commanded for certain days of the year
FIRST TEMPLE	The Temple built by King Solomon, but which was destroyed by the Babylonians in 586 B.C.E.
GALUT	Place of exile, away from one's land. The first exile was in Babylonia, after 586 B.C.E. and the next great one, after 70 C.E. following Roman conquest of Judea
GEDALIAH	Governor of Jerusalem following Judea's defeat by the Babylonians in 586 B.C.E. His murder plunged Jews into deep sorrow and grief
GREAT EXILE	The exile that followed Roman defeat of Jews in 70 C.E., when the Jews were scattered all over the known world
HAFTORAH	The portion from the Prophets read on Sabbaths and festivals as it relates to the Torah portion of that day
HAZON	"Vision," the name given to the Sabbath before Tisha B'Av
ISAIAH	The first of the Major Prophets. Also refers to the "Second Isaiah" who lived during the days of the Babylonian Exile
JEREMIAH	The second of the Major Prophets, who lived during the time of the destruction of the First Temple
KINGDOM OF JUDAH	The southern of the two divided Kingdoms, following the death of Solomon, which was conquered by the Babylonians
KINOT	Special prayers of mourning and deep sadness read on the morning of Tisha B'Av
MAJOR FAST	A fast lasting from evening to evening
MESSIAH	The descendant of David who will come, in due time, to bring the Jews of the world back to their homeland, Israel
MINOR FAST	A fast that lasts from sunrise to sunset of same day
MORDECAI	A famous Jew, cousin of Esther, whom he adopted—hero of the story of Purim

NEBUCHADNEZZAR	King of Babylonia who conquered the Jews in 586 B.C.E.
NINTH OF AV	English name for Tisha B'Av
SABBATH OF COMFORTING	English name for Shabbat Nahamu. Also, refers to the "Seven Sabbaths of Comfort" which follow the Fast of Av
SABBATHS OF REBUKE	The three Sabbaths before the Fast of Av, when we read the portions from the Prophets who rebuke the Israelites for their sins
SECOND TEMPLE	The Temple that was rebuilt by the Jews returning from the Babylonian Exile, completed in 516 B.C.E.
SEVENTEENTH OF TAMMUZ	The Fast commemorating the first breach in the walls of Jerusalem, which led to its destruction
SHABBAT HAZON	The Sabbath before Tisha B'Av, so named from the first word of haftorah of that day
SHABBAT NAHAMU	"Sabbath of Comfort," so named from the opening word of the haftorah of that day, where Prophet seeks to comfort the Jews
SIX-DAY WAR	The war against the Arabs which Israel fought and won in June, 1967
TA'ANIT B'CHORIM	Hebrew name for "Fast of the First-born"
TAMMUZ	The fourth month of the Hebrew year, when a fast occurs on the 17th
TEFILLIN	Phylacteries (two little black boxes with straps attached) worn by Jewish men during morning weekday services
TENTH OF TEVET	Fast-day in memory of the day when the Babylonians first besieged Jerusalem
TEVET	Tenth month of the Hebrew year, on the 10th of which a fast occurs
TISHA B'AV	The Ninth of Av when the "Black Fast" falls in memory of the destruction of both the First and the Second Temples; a major fast
YOM KIPPUR	Day of Atonement, on the 10th of Tishri, the holiest day of the year; a major fast

NUMBERS RELATED TO THE JEWISH FAST-DAYS

1   All fasts last *one* day or less
    The Fast of the *First*-born comes in Nissan, the *first* month of the year

2   The *Second* Temple was destroyed on Tisha B'Av, in year 70 C.E.

3. The *three* Sabbaths of Rebuke come before the Fast of Av
    There are *three* weeks between the Fast of Tammuz and the Fast of Av
    The Fast of Gedaliah comes on the *third* of Tishri
    Esther fasted for *three* days before going to see the king

4   Tammuz is the *fourth* month of the year

5   Av is the *fifth* month of the year

7   There are *seven* Sabbaths of Comforting following the Fast of Av
    Tishri is the *seventh* month of the year, when the Fast of Gedaliah and Yom Kippur come

9   The Fast of Av is on the *ninth* of that month
    The first *nine* days of Av are the saddest of all

10 The Fast of Tevet is on the *tenth* of that month
    Tevet is the *tenth* month of the year
    Yom Kippur is on the *tenth* of Tishri

12 The Fast of Esther falls in Adar, the *twelfth* month of the year

13 The Fast of Esther falls on the *thirteenth* day of Adar

14 The Fast of the First-born falls on the *fourteenth* day of Nissan

17 The Fast of Tammuz falls on the *seventeenth* day of that month

40 The Israelites wandered in the desert for *forty* years

70 The Second Temple was destroyed on Tisha B'Av in *70* C.E.

135 Betar, the last Jewish stronghold, fell to the Romans in the year *135* C.E.

586 The First Temple was destroyed on Tisha B'Av, in *586* B.C.E.

1492 The Jews were expelled from Spain on Tisha B'Av in *1492*

1914 The beginning of World War I was on Tisha B'Av in *1914*

QUIZ QUESTIONS FOR THE JEWISH FAST-DAYS

QUESTIONS:

1. The term "Tisha B'Av" means

2. Why do we observe it?

3. During what year, and by whom, was each Temple destroyed?

4. The year 70 C.E. was a tragic year for the Jews. Why?

5. a) What is meant by the "Three Weeks"?
   b) When do they begin and end?

6. The "Nine Days" refer to

7. Why is the 17th of Tammuz a day of fasting and sadness?

8. How do we show our feelings of sadness during the Nine Days?

9. It is Tisha B'Av night. What is different in the synagogue?

10. Which two special books are read on Tisha B'Av, and when is each one read?

11. What is *Shabbat Nahamu?*

ANSWERS:

1. The Ninth day of the month of Av

2. As a reminder of the destruction of the First and Second Temples

3. The First in 586 B.C.E. by the Babylonians; the Second, in 70 C.E. by the Romans

4. The Temple was destroyed, thus beginning the Great Exile and loss of Jewish nationality

5. a) The Three Weeks which come just before the Ninth of Av
   b) From the 17th of Tammuz through the Ninth of Av

6. The first nine days of the month of Av, ending with Tisha B'Av

7. Mainly, because on that day the Babylonians had made the first breach in the walls of Jerusalem

8. No meat, no wine, no swimming, no weddings or other celebrations or festivities are permitted

9. Lights are dim; worshippers sit on the floor or on stools; they wear no leather footwear; the *Parochet* (the Ark curtain) is removed; all speak in low tones

10. Book of Lamentations at night; and Kinot (special mournful prayers) the following morning

11. The "Sabbath of Consolation," immediately following Tisha B'Av

12. When are the Talis and Tefillin worn on Tisha B'Av?

13. What do the two fasts, Tisha B'Av and Yom Kippur, have in common?

14. a) Are we to be sad on every fast-day?
    b) On which are we not sad?

15. a) What is meant by a "Major" fast?
    b) A "Minor" fast?
    c) Give an example of each.

16. Which of the fast days do we observe:
    a) because of a national tragedy?
    b) as a plea to God to save us from death?
    c) by not fasting?

17. Give an example of a special fast.

18. a) Name a few sad events that occurred on Tisha B'Av.
    b) By what other special name is Tisha B'Av known?
    c) Why?

19. a) Will Tisha B'Av ever be abolished?
    b) Explain.

20. Why is the 10th of Tevet a day of fasting?

12. Only during Mincha (afternoon) service, instead of the morning

13. Both are major fasts, when fasting lasts for 24 hours, from evening to evening

14. a) No
    b) On Yom Kippur and Ta'anit B'chorim (Fast of the First-born)

15. a) One that lasts from evening to evening
    b) One lasting from sunrise to sunset
    c) Major—Yom Kippur and Tisha B'Av
       Minor—10th of Tevet and all others

16. a) 10th of Tevet, Fast of Tammuz, 9th of Av, Tzom Gedaliah
    b) Fast of Esther
    c) Fast of the First-born

17. Bride and groom on their wedding day; the Six-Day War

18. a) Jews were expelled from Spain in 1492; the Israelites had to wander in the desert for 40 years; World War I began
    b) The Black Fast
    c) All the above and other events occurred on this day

19. a) Yes, some day in the future
    b) This will take place when the Messiah will come

20. The Babylonians began to besiege Jerusalem

21. In addition to the reason given in No. 7 (above) give a few other reasons for observing the Fast of Tammuz.

22. Give the date and reason for the Fast of Gedaliah.

23. a) When does the Fast of Esther come?
    b) Why do we fast on that day?

24. a) What is meant by *Ta'anit B'chorim?*
    b) Why should it be a day of fasting?
    c) How do we avoid fasting on that day?

25. a) Name three basic reasons for fasting.
    b) Give an example of each.
    c) Also, give an example of a "special fast".
    d) Why was there a fast during the Six-Day War?

26. a) When a fast falls on a Sabbath, which fasts are, and which ones are not, observed on that day?
    b) In such a case, when is the fast observed?

27. a) On which days of the week can the Fast of Esther never be observed?
    b) Why not?
    c) When is it then observed?

21. Moses broke the Tablets of the Ten Commandments; daily Temple sacrifices stopped; Apostomus placed an idol in the Temple

22. The 3rd of Tishri; murder of Gedaliah, a well-liked Jewish governor

23. a) On the 13th of Adar (day before Purim)
    b) To remind us that Esther fasted before she went to the king to beg for the lives of the Jews

24. a) The Fast of the First-born
    b) As thanks to God for having saved the Hebrew first-born children from the Angel of Death
    c) By studying and completing a portion from the Talmud

25. a) Forgiveness of sins; reminder of national tragedy; prayer for God's help in time of trouble
    b) Yom Kippur; Tisha B'Av; Fast of Esther
    c) Bride and groom before their wedding; every Friday until Sabbath
    d) To ask divine help for an Israeli victory

26. a) Only Yom Kippur may be observed on the Sabbath
    b) All others (except Fast of Esther) are postponed for the following day

27. a) Friday, Saturday or Sunday
    b) No fast other than Yom Kippur is permitted on the Sabbath
    c) On the Thursday before

28. Correct the following sentence: All our fasts will be practiced forever.

29. Name at least two ways that fasting makes one a better Jew.

30. a) Who is required to fast?
    b) Who must not fast?
    c) How can a child under age 13 try to fast?

28. All fasts, except Yom Kippur, will be abolished when the Messiah will come

29. Reminds us of the reason for fasting; brings our past history to mind; brings us closer to our people; gives us more hope and courage to face life as a Jew

30. a) Every Jew, 13 years of age or over, who is in good health
    b) Anyone too sick, too weak, or too old to fast
    c) On fast-days, avoid eating unnecessary foods, such as candy, gum, etc.
       Also, eat meals at a later time than usual

ROSH HODESH

Did you know that we Jews have a holiday not only every week (Sabbath) but also every month? It is a minor festival known as *Rosh Hodesh*, "the head of the month." (Compare with *Rosh HaShana*, "the head of the year.")

It is observed every month (except for the month of Tishri) for either one or two days. Why do we observe it? The Bible (Numbers 28:11-15) commands us to honor it as a holy day. But, since work is not forbidden on this day, Rosh Hodesh is a minor festival. In ancient times the first day of the month was determined by observing the moon and then making a public announcement accompanied by the sounding of the Shofar.

HOW DO WE OBSERVE ROSH HODESH?

According to our Hebrew calendar, which is based on the movements of the moon, every month has either 29 or 30 days. When an outgoing month has 30 days, two days of Rosh Hodesh are observed—the thirtieth of the old month and the first of the new one. If however there are only 29 days in the old month, then only one day is observed—the first of the new month. Thus, if the month of Sivan contains 30 days, the 30th of Sivan is the first day of Rosh Hodesh and the first of Tammuz, the second day.

On the Sabbath before Rosh Hodesh (*Shabbat M'varchim*) a special prayer, called the "Blessing of the New Moon," is recited, when the name of the new month is announced as well as the days on which it will fall during the coming week. Then, on Rosh Hodesh itself, special prayers, including the *Hallel,* are recited and the Torah is read.

Today, Rosh Hodesh is only a half-holiday, but in ancient times it was celebrated as a major festival. In the Temple, special sacrifices were offered and it was a day for family gatherings and feasts, for visiting the prophet, and for other celebrations. Let us remember this ancient festival as it comes each month.

TERMS FOR ROSH HODESH

BLESSING OF THE NEW MONTH	The prayer recited on the Sabbath before Rosh Hodesh, announcing its coming
ROSH HODESH	Beginning of the month
SHABBAT M'VARCHIM	Hebrew for "Sabbath of Blessing (of the New Moon)"
TISHRI	The month in which Rosh Hodesh is not observed

NUMBERS RELATING TO ROSH HODESH

1 *First* of the month is Rosh Hodesh

2 Sometimes Rosh Hodesh is observed for *two* days

29 Some Hebrew months have *29* days

30 In some months there are *30* days

QUIZ QUESTIONS FOR ROSH HODESH

1. What is the difference between "Rosh Hodesh" and "Rosh HaShana"?

2. a) For how many days is Rosh Hodesh observed?
   b) How is this determined?

3. Why is Rosh Hodesh a minor festival?

4. a) When do we announce the coming of the new month?
   b) What is announced at that time?
   c) By what name is this Sabbath called?

5. How is Rosh Hodesh observed today?

6. How was Rosh Hodesh observed in ancient times?

7. a) In what manner was the beginning of a month determined during ancient times?
   b) How was it publicly announced?

8. a) In which month is Rosh Hodesh not celebrated?
   b) Why not?

---

1. Rosh Hodesh—the beginning of the month; Rosh HaShana—the beginning of the New Year

2. a) One or two days
   b) If the old month has 30 days—two are observed; if 29—only one day

3. The Biblical commandment does not forbid work on this day

4. a) The Sabbath before Rosh Hodesh
   b) The name of the new month and the days of Rosh Hodesh
   c) *Shabbat Mevor'chim*, or, "Sabbath of Blessing (of the New Moon)"

5. By special prayers, Torah reading

6. By family gatherings and feasts, visits to the prophet, special Temple offerings

7. a) By observing the moon
   b) By sounding the Shofar

8. a) Tishri
   b) Because Rosh HaShana (New Year) falls on the first of that month

THE HEBREW CALENDAR

Hebrew Month	Corresponding Month	Festival	Hebrew Date
NISSAN	March-April	Passover	15-22
IYAR	April-May	Israel Independence Day	5
		Lag B'Omer	18
SIVAN	May-June	Shavuot	6-7
TAMMUZ	June-July	Fast of Tammuz	17
AV	July-August	Fast of Av	9
ELUL	August-September	—	—
TISHRI	September-October	Rosh HaShana	1-2
		Yom Kippur	10
		Sukkot, Sh'mini Atzeret and Simhat Torah	15-23
HESHVAN	October-November	—	—
KISLEV	November-December	Hanukka	25 through
TEVET	December-January	(last few days of Hanukka)	2 or 3*
SHVAT	January-February	Tu Bishvat	15
ADAR	February-March	Purim**	14
ADAR SHENI (Adar II)	(Comes only during a leap year)		

*When Kislev has 29 days, Hanukka ends on the 3rd of Tevet, but when there are 30 days in Kislev it ends on the 2nd.
**During a leap year Purim falls in Adar II.

FOR FURTHER READING

Cohen, M. J., *Pathways Through the Bible*
Edidin, B. M., *Jewish Holidays and Festivals*
Epstein, M., *All About Jewish Holidays and Customs*
Essrig, H. and Segal, A., *Israel Today*
Feder, S. and Bialik, M., *Yom Ha'Atzmaut (Israeli Independence Day)*
Gamoran, M., *Days and Ways*
Gamoran, M., *Hillel's Happy Holidays*
Golub, R., *Down Holiday Lane*
Goodman, P., *The Passover Anthology*
Goodman, P., *The Purim Anthology*
Goodman, P., *The Rosh HaShanah Anthology*
Goodman, P., *The Yom Kippur Anthology*
Greenstone, J., *Jewish Feasts and Fasts*
Hertz, J. H., *The Pentateuch and the Haftorahs*
Hoffman, G., *The Land and People of Israel*
Idelsohn, A. Z., *Ceremonies of Judaism*
Ish-Kishor, S., *Pathways Through the Jewish Holidays*
Jacobs, L., *A Guide to Rosh HaShanah*
Jacobs, L., *A Guide to Yom Kippur*
Levinger, E. E., *Jewish Holidays*
Levinger, E. E., *Jewish Holyday Stories*
Levinger, E. E., *With the Jewish Child in Home and Synagogue*
Louvish, M., *The Challenge of Israel*
Millgram, A., *Sabbath, The Day of Delight*
Schauss, H., *Jewish Festivals*
Segal, S. M., *The Sabbath Book*
Seidman, H., *The Glory of the Jewish Holidays*
Sperling, I., *Reasons for Jewish Customs and Traditions*
Vainstein, Y., *The Cycle of the Jewish Year*
Weilerstein, R., *The Adventures of K'Tonton*
Weilerstein, R., *What Danny Did*
Weilerstein, R., *What the Moon Brought*
Zeligs, D., *The Story of Jewish Holidays and Customs*

INDEX

Abraham 34, 46, 106
Adar 93, 94, 99, 101, 104
Ad-lo-ya-dah 99, 104
Afikoman 110, 111, 116, 117
Ahad Ha'am 22, 30
Ahasuerus, King 93, 98, 99, 100, 103, 166
Akdamot 150, 154, 159
Akiba, Rabbi 120, 138, 141, 142, 143, 144, 146
Al Ha-Nisim 69, 75, 80, 95, 99, 101
Al Heyt 41, 43
Aliyah, Aliyot 18, 23, 59, 60
Aliyah (to Israel) 23, 86, 87, 90, 126
Amalekites 95, 99, 101, 104
Amnon, Rabbi 38, 47
Antiochus 68, 75, 79
Arabs 69, 121, 122, 123, 124, 126, 133, 134
Aramaic 18, 23, 27
Aravot 54, 57, 60, 63, 64
Atonement. See Yom Kippur
Avodah 42, 43, 49
Baal Tokeah 38, 43, 46
Babylonia, Babylonians 40, 165, 166, 169, 172, 173, 175, 176
Balfour Declaration 122, 124, 126, 129, 134
Bar Kochba 120, 137, 141, 143
Bar Mitzva 18, 28, 60
Basle (Switzerland) 122, 126, 129, 133
Besamim 19, 23, 28 (spices, 28)
Bible 14, 15, 23, 24, 29, 34, 37, 53, 54, 82, 84, 92, 94, 99, 103, 108, 117, 129, 137, 138, 139, 141, 148, 150, 151, 155, 156, 158, 179
Bible Quiz, International 127, 129
Bikkurim (offerings) 151, 152, 154, 159
Birkat Ha-Mazon 18, 23
Bitter Herbs. See Maror
"Black Fast" 165, 171, 176. See also Tisha B'Av and Fast of Av
Book of Life 33, 35, 36, 37, 39, 40, 50
Bow and Arrow 140, 141, 144, 146
Choni Ha-ma'agel 86, 87, 89
B'rit Millah 168, 171
Confession 36, 41, 42, 49
Dairy foods 152, 160
David, King 149, 150, 154, 155, 159, 160, 172
Dreidl 69, 70, 75, 77
Egypt 14, 23, 26, 53, 95, 102, 106, 107, 109, 111, 112, 113, 114, 116, 118, 148, 157, 165, 166, 171
Eleazar 72, 75
Elijah, Cup of 112, 116
Elul 37, 43, 47
Emek 89
Erev Pesah 111, 114
Erev Shabbat 17, 22, 23, 24, 25
Esther, Queen 93, 95, 97, 98, 99, 100, 102, 103, 104, 172, 174
  Book of, Megilla of 92, 94, 95, 96, 99, 100, 103
  Fast of 96, 100, 101, 104, 166, 167, 168, 170, 176, 177

184

INDEX

Ethrog 52, 54, 57, 58, 60, 63, 64
Exiles 126, 164, 171, 172, 175
Exodus (from Egypt) 14, 23, 106, 107, 110, 111, 112, 148, 165, 171
   Book of 108, 109, 117, 148, 150
Fast, of Av 20, 167, 168, 170, 171, 172, 173. See also Tisha B'Av
   of Esther 96, 164, 167, 168, 170, 171, 174, 176, 177
   of the First-born (Ta'anit B'chorim) 164, 166, 170, 171, 173, 174, 176, 177
   of Gedaliah (Tzom Gedaliah) 40, 44, 164, 166, 167, 170, 171, 174
   of Tammuz 164, 165, 167, 168, 170, 173, 174, 175, 176, 177
   of Tevet 164, 165, 167, 170, 173, 176
   private or special 164, 167, 176, 177
Fast Days: Major 163, 164, 167, 168, 170, 172, 176
   Minor 163, 164, 165, 167, 170, 172, 176
Fasting 17, 36, 40, 41, 49, 50, 93, 161-181
First Fruits, Festival of. See Bikkurim, Shavuot
Five Scrolls 94, 95, 99, 100
Four Questions 109, 110, 111
Four Species 54, 57, 60, 61, 63
Fourth Commandment 14, 16, 23, 25, 26
Ghettoes 120, 129, 132
G'mar Hatimah Tovah 40, 42, 43, 50

Great Britain 122, 123, 129, 134
Greek, Greeks 68, 71, 75, 79, 80
Grogger 95, 99
Hadassim 54, 57, 60, 63, 64
Had Gadya 111, 116, 118
Hadrian 137, 141
Haftorah 18, 20, 23, 28, 29, 40, 168, 169, 172
Haganah 123, 126, 129, 134
Haggadah 108, 110, 111, 113, 116, 118
Hag Ha-Asif 54, 60, 64, 66
Hag Ha Bikkurim (Shavuot) 149, 154
Hag Ha-Matzot (Passover) 111, 114
Hag Ha-Sukkot 54, 60, 66
Hakafah, Hakafot 58, 59, 60, 66
Halla 14, 17, 23, 25, 26, 39, 47
Hallel 57, 69, 75, 80, 127, 129, 180
Halutz, Halutzim 84, 86, 121, 126, 129, 133
Haman 93, 94, 95, 97, 98, 99, 100, 103, 104, 166, 171
Hametz 108, 111, 114, 115, 116, 117, 118
Hammentash 95, 99, 100, 101, 109
Ha-motzi 21, 23
Ha-Nerot Halalu 69, 75, 80
Hannah 71, 75, 77, 80
Hanukka 67-80, 93, 99
Hanukka Gelt 70, 75, 79
Hanukkiah 75
Harosset 109, 111, 116, 117
Hattan B'reshit 59, 60, 66
Hattan Torah 59, 60, 66

185

INDEX

Havdala 19, 23, 28
Herzl, Theodor 86, 89, 122, 126, 129, 133
High Holy Days 20, 31-33, 36-38, 40-47, 53, 58, 60
High Priest 35, 50, 68, 75, 79
Hillel 73
Hol Ha-Moed 54, 58, 60, 108, 110, 111, 114
Hoshana, Hoshanot 54, 57, 58, 60, 64
Hoshana Rabba 54, 58, 60, 62, 63, 64
Huppah 84, 86, 88
Independence Day (Yom Ha'-Atzmaut) 119-135, 136, 145, 146
Israel 22, 23, 34, 35, 55, 58, 65, 68, 84, 86, 87, 88, 89, 102, 104, 113, 114, 115, 120, 121, 122, 126, 135, 145, 147, 148, 164, 183
Israel Bonds 86, 90
Israel Independence Day. See Independence Day
Iyar 129, 131, 132, 140, 142, 143
Jerusalem 42, 43, 50, 53, 54, 68, 75, 82, 86, 87, 90, 126, 128, 137, 152, 155, 165, 170, 173, 175, 176
Jewish National Fund 86, 88, 89
Jonah 42, 50
Judah Maccabee 68, 73, 74, 75, 76, 78
Kabbalat Shabbat 17, 23, 24
Kapparot 40, 43
Kiddush 17, 18, 20, 24, 27, 39, 116

Kinot 168, 172, 175
Kislev 73, 75, 77, 78
Kittel 41, 58, 60
Kol Ha-n'arim 59, 66
Kol Nidre 41, 43, 49
Lag B'Omer 120, 125, 132, 136, 146
Latkes 70, 74, 75, 79
L'cha Dodi 17, 24, 27
L'Shanah Tovah Tikateyvu 32, 37, 43
Lulav 52, 54, 57, 58, 60, 63, 64
Maccabee, Maccabean 69, 75, 76, 80. See also Judah Maccabee
Mah Nishtanah ("Four Questions") 112
Malchiot 38, 43, 47
Manna 14, 24, 26
Maot Hittim 112, 117
Maoz Tzur 69, 75, 80
Maftir 18
Mandate, British 122, 123, 126, 129, 134
Maror (Bitter Herbs) 109, 111, 112, 116
Mattathias 68, 72, 74, 75, 76, 77, 78
Matza, Matzot 108-113
Megilla (reading) 94, 95, 96, 99, 101, of Ruth 150, 154
Melavah Malkah 19, 24, 28
Memorial Day. See Yom Ha-Zikaron
Menora 68, 73, 75
Messiah 149, 150, 154, 165, 172, 176, 178
Middle Ages 83, 120, 129, 132
Minha 18, 24, 42, 50

INDEX

Minor Festivals 79, 139, 181
Mishloach Manot 95, 99, 100, 101, 104
Modin 68, 76, 79
Mordecai 80, 93, 94, 97, 99, 100, 103, 104, 166, 172
Moses 14, 69, 79, 106, 111, 166, 177
Motzaey Shabbat 24
Mount Sinai 34, 148, 150, 152, 154, 157, 160
Mussaf 24, 27, 29, 38, 41, 43, 44, 45, 47, 49, 50
Myrtles. See Hadassim
Nazis 122, 126, 134
Neilah 42, 43, 50
New Year (for trees) 86. See also Tu Bishvat
Nissan 34, 106, 112, 113, 114, 170, 174
Nun, Gimmel, Hay, Shin 69, 76, 77, 79
Oil 68, 79
Omer, Counting of 111-114, 138, 140, 141-144, 149, 151, 154, 156, 160
Oneg Shabbat 24, 28
Oral Law 120, 129, 130, 132, 141, 148, 150, 155, 160. See also Talmud
Oshpizin 56, 60
Palestine (Israel) 122, 123, 124, 126, 129, 130, 134
Pascal Lamb 108, 112, 116
Passover 20, 33, 34, 53, 61, 64, 105-118, 128, 138, 139, 141, 143, 144, 145, 148, 149, 151, 156, 157, 160

Penitence, Days of 32, 33, 40, 43, 44, 45
Persia 93, 98, 99, 100, 101, 102
Prophet, Phophets 14, 18, 20, 23, 24, 28, 42, 50, 172
Purim 91-104, 166, 171, 172, 177
  Legends of 97-98
  Other days of 96
  Shushan 96, 100, 101, 103
Queen, Sabbath 16, 18, 26
Rain, Prayer for (T'filat Geshem) 55, 58, 61, 65
Red Sea, Miracle of 20, 110, 113, 118
Rishon L'Tzion 122, 130, 133
Rome, Romans 120, 126, 132, 137, 138, 141, 142, 143, 145, 146, 165, 169, 170, 172, 174, 175
Rosh HaShana 29, 31-40, 43-49, 82, 88, 166, 171, 181
Rosh HaShana L'Ilanot (Tu Bishvat) 82, 86, 88
Rosh Hodesh 24, 179-181
Ruth 154, 155, 160
  Book of 149, 150, 159
Sabbath 11-30, 37, 39, 43, 44, 46, 55, 57, 61, 69, 72, 80, 96, 108, 167, 169, 177, 179, 180, 181
Sabbath of Rebuke. See Shabbat Hazon
S'chach 56, 61, 63
Seder 108, 110-112, 114, 116, 118
Seder Plate 109, 111-113, 116, 118
Sedra, Sedrot 18, 24, 25, 27, 55, 59, 61
Seudah (for Purim) 95, 100, 101
Seudah Sh'lishit 18, 24, 28

187

INDEX

S'firah 112, 138, 140, 150, 155
Shabbat Ha-Gadol 20, 28, 29, 112, 114
Shabbat Hazon 20, 29, 168, 172, 173
Shabbat M'varchim 20, 24, 29, 180, 181
Shabbat Nachamu 20, 29, 169, 173, 175
Shabbat Shalom 17, 24, 27
Shabbat Shira 20, 28, 29
Shabbat Shuva 20, 28, 29, 40, 44
Shacharit 24, 27, 50
Shalom Aleichem 17, 20, 24, 27
Shalosh Regalim (the Three Festivals) 53, 61, 64, 112, 114, 148, 155
Shammash 69, 74, 76, 77, 78
Shavuot 53, 61, 64, 107, 110, 112, 128, 138, 141, 143, 144, 147-160
Shehecheyanu 39
Sh'mini Atzeret 53, 54, 55, 58, 61, 62, 65
Shofar 34, 37, 38, 42, 43, 44, 45, 46, 47, 50, 181
Shofrot 38, 44, 47
Shushan 93, 94, 100, 101, 102, Purim in, 96, 100, 101
Sh'varim 38, 44, 46
Shvat 82, 87, 88
Simeon bar Yohai 138, 140, 141, 142, 143, 144, 145
Simhat Bet Ha-Shoevah 58, 61, 64
Simhat Torah 53, 54, 55, 58, 59, 60, 61, 62, 66
Sivan 150, 155, 156, 157

Six-Day War 69, 83, 124, 126, 131, 135, 164, 167, 173, 177
S'lihot 37, 44
Spain 120, 130, 132, 165, 174, 176
State of Israel 83, 87, 89, 90, 120, 123, 124, 126, 127, 130, 131, 134, 146
Sukka 52, 53, 54, 56, 60, 61, 63
Sukkot, Festival of 51-66, 73, 79, 88, 107, 112, 128, 148
Syria, Syrians 68, 71, 72, 74, 75, 76, 78, 79, 80
Ta'anit B'chorim (Fast of the First-Born) 164, 166, 173, 176, 177
Ta'anit Esther. See Fast of Esther
Talit 59, 66, 176
Talmud 32, 56, 61, 120, 130, 132, 141, 159, 160, 177. See also Oral Law
Tashlich 38, 44, 47
Tefillin 173, 176
Tel Aviv 86, 87, 90
Temple 26, 38, 40, 41, 43, 47, 49, 53, 54, 56, 57, 58, 61, 68, 73, 75, 79, 82, 86, 112, 116, 126, 128, 137, 138, 139, 141, 143, 144, 151, 152, 154, 159, 164, 165, 166, 168, 170, 171, 172, 173, 174, 180, 181
Ten Commandments 14, 25, 26, 34, 46, 147, 148, 150, 153, 154, 155, 156, 157, 158, 159, 160, 166, 177
Teneh 151, 155, 159
Ten Plagues 112, 118

INDEX

Three Days of Preparation 150, 155, 156, 160
(The) Three Festivals. See Shalosh Regalim
Tikkun 150, 155, 159
Tisha B'Av (Ninth of Av) 163, 164-169, 171, 172, 173, 174, 175, 176, 177
Tishri 29, 34, 37, 44, 45, 46, 49, 53, 61, 62, 63, 166, 170, 173, 174, 177, 179, 180
Tithe 82, 86, 89
T'kiah 38, 44, 46
Torah 14, 18, 23, 24, 25, 27, 29, 34, 35, 36, 38, 41, 45, 48, 49, 52, 53, 55, 56, 58, 59, 60, 61, 65, 66, 69, 87, 98, 107, 110, 117, 118, 120, 125, 126, 132, 135, 136, 137, 140, 141, 142, 143, 144, 145, 146, 148, 149, 150, 152, 155, 156, 157, 158, 160, 168, 180, 181
Trees 98
  New Year for 81, 82, 83
  Planting in Israel 84, 88, 89
  Certificates 84, 88
  In Bible 84
T'ruah 38, 44, 46
Tu Bishvat 20, 29, 81-90
Turkish Empire (also Ottoman) 122, 130

Unetaneh Tokef 38, 44, 47
United Nations 123, 124, 126, 134, 135
Vashti 93, 97, 98, 100, 102
"Wandering Jew" 120, 130, 132
Weizmann, Chaim 86, 87, 89, 122, 124, 126, 130, 134
Willows. See Aravot
World War I 122, 126, 133, 134, 165, 174, 176
World Zionist Congress 122, 126, 129, 130, 133
Yizkor 55, 58, 61, 65, 110, 112, 115, 150
Yom Ha'Atzmaut. See Independence Day
Yom Ha-Din 34, 44, 46, 48
Yom Ha-Zikaron 34, 44, 46, 48
  In Israel 127, 129, 130
Yom Kippur 17, 29, 31-33, 35-38, 40-47, 49, 50, 96, 163, 164, 167, 169, 170, 173, 174, 176, 177, 178
Yom T'ruah 34, 37, 44, 46, 48
Zemirot 12, 18, 22, 25, 27
Zichronot 38, 44, 47
Zionism 86, 87, 89, 122, 126, 130, 133
Z'man Simhateynu 54, 61, 64, 66

J
S
235
GO

Golomb, Morris.
 Know your festivals and enjoy them

DATE DUE			
JAN 22 '80			
NOV 1 6 '80			
JAN 1 0 '83			
MAY 21 '85			
JAN 7 '89			

BETH HILLEL LIBRARY
WILMETTE, ILLINOIS

WITHDRAWN